Lisa Marie Bopp

Awesome Facts for Potter Fans

The Unofficial Advent Calendar

Incredible Facts, Trivia Games, Recipes & Lots of Surprises

© 2024 Nucleo
Edition 1.0A

Author:
Lisa Marie Bopp

Publisher:
Nucleo – a label of
my dna media GmbH
Ohmstr. 53
60486 Frankfurt am Main,
Germany

ISBN:
978-3-98561-064-8

Feedback, Questions, Suggestions?

Get in touch with us at **info@nucleo-media.com** or visit our homepage **nucleo-media.com**

Time for Magical Moments!

Christmas isn't just celebrated in the Muggle world — witches and wizards get in on the fun, too!

Enter the magical world of Christmas and immerse yourself in the magic throughout the month of December.

This special kind of Advent calendar will surprise you every day with incredible facts from the world of magic. You can also look forward to tricky quizzes, fun games and even recipes to try.

Get ready for a magical pre-Christmas season of fun that lasts right up until New Year's Eve!

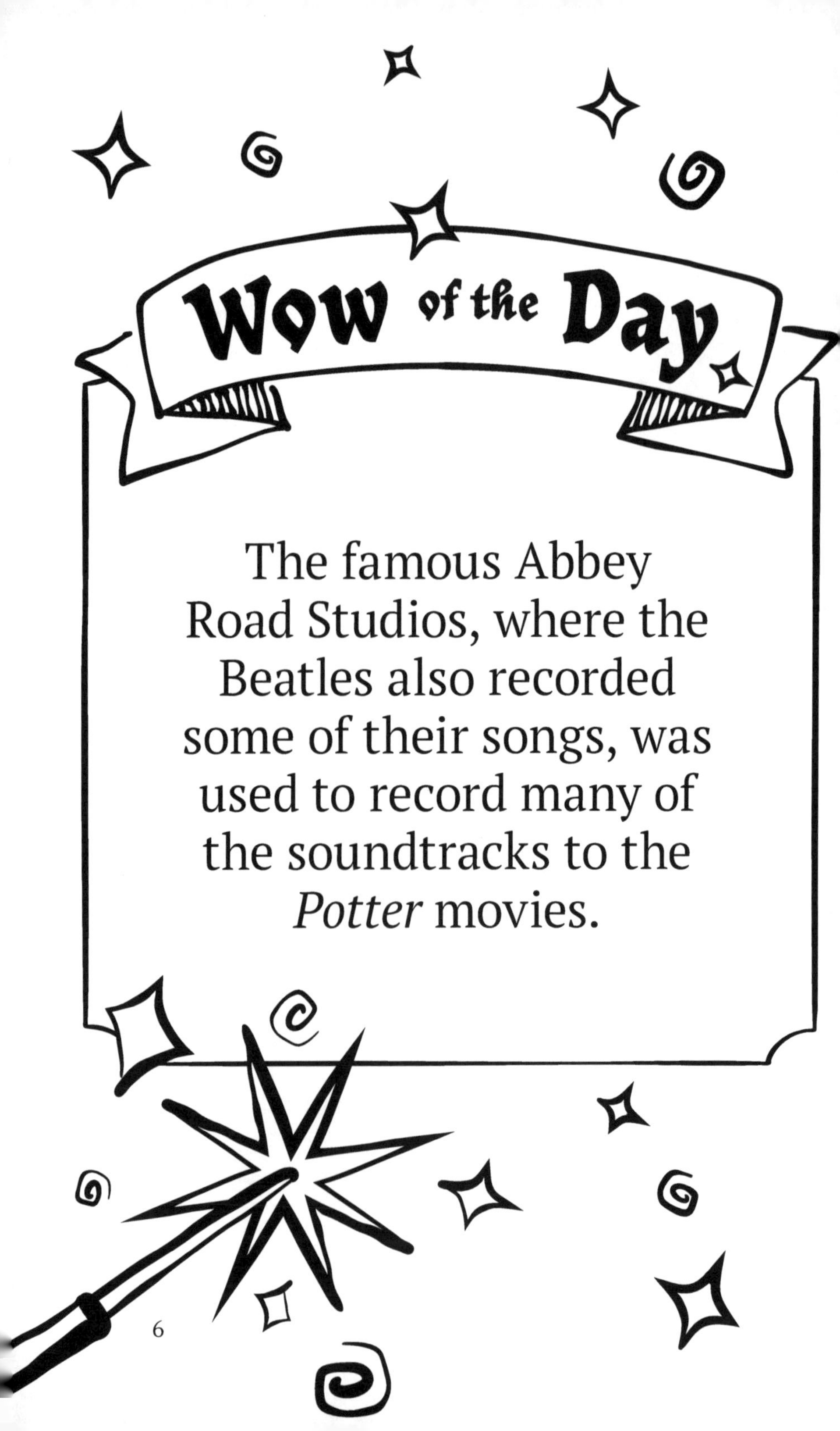

The famous Abbey Road Studios, where the Beatles also recorded some of their songs, was used to record many of the soundtracks to the *Potter* movies.

The Fitting Challenge

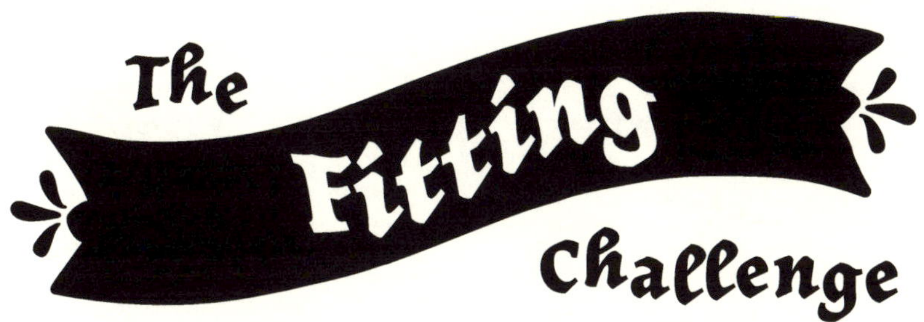

Something seems to have slipped into the books of spells here. Can you see which actually non-existing spell has crept in? Circle it.

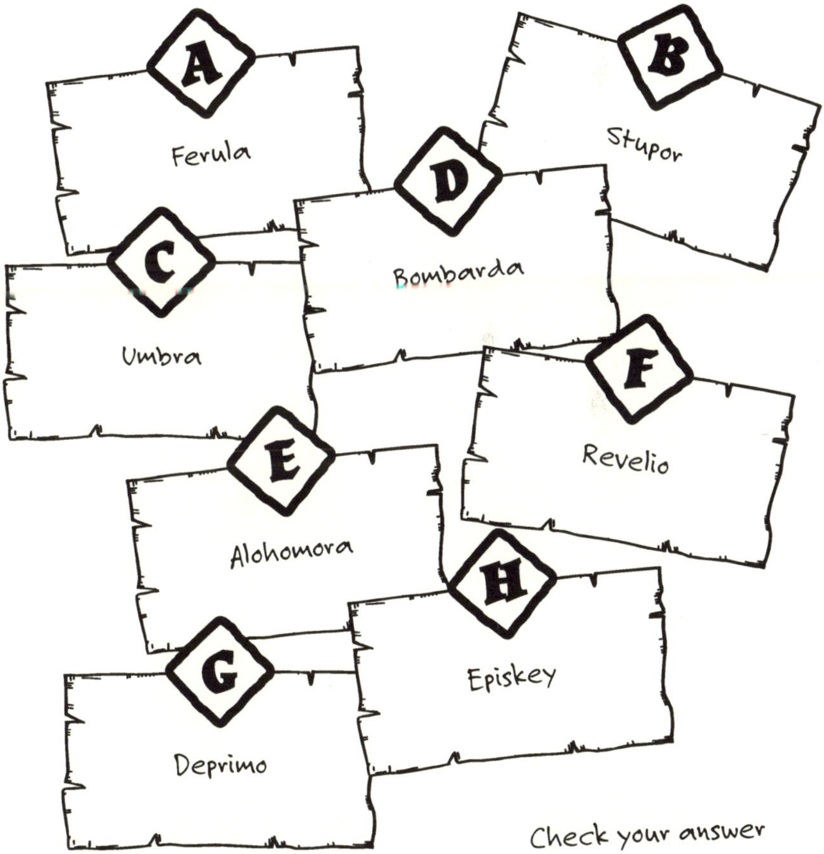
A
Ferula
B
Stupor
D
Bombarda
C
Umbra
F
Revelio
E
Alohomora
H
Episkey
G
Deprimo

Check your answer on the next page.

There are numerous spells to learn in *Harry Potter*. Yet, Umbra is not one of them (answer C). In Germany, the translation of the *Potter* books has even led to a completely new spell. In the wizarding world, the spell Obliviate is normally used to erase the memory of a Muggle, a witch, or a wizard. It can be applied to completely erase all memories or just selected ones. However, the German translation introduced an additional spell called Amnesia to differentiate between Obliviate — the partial erasure — and Amnesia — the complete erasure. The English original does not make this distinction.

Did You Know That ...

... Lupin actor David Thewlis had to spend six hours in the make-up chair to become a werewolf?

... the famous Fabergé eggs were the inspiration for the golden egg in *Harry Potter and the Goblet of Fire*?

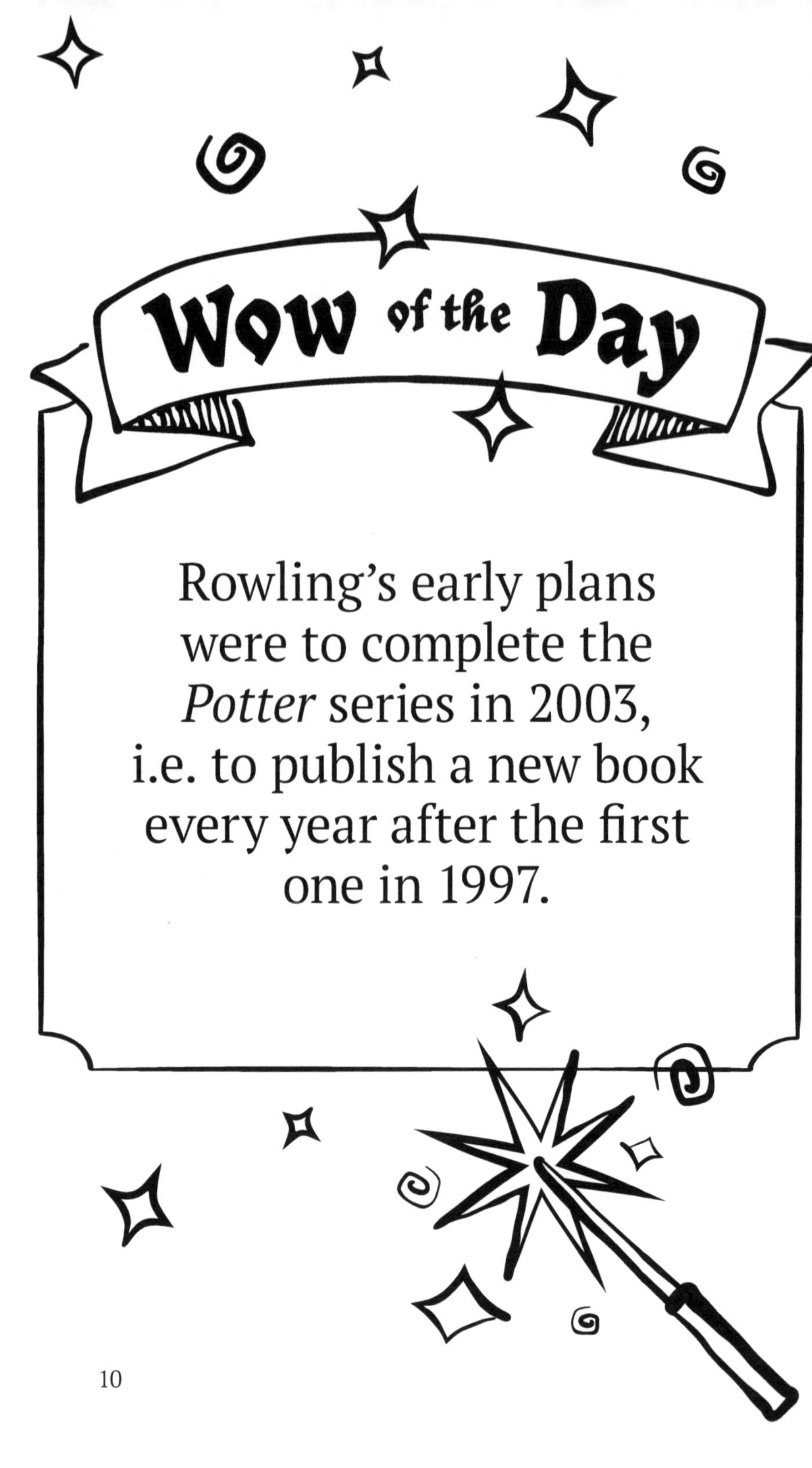

Rowling's early plans were to complete the *Potter* series in 2003, i.e. to publish a new book every year after the first one in 1997.

Magic Potions

House Drink of the Yellow House

Known for their loyalty and sense of justice, the members of the House of the badger can also be tempted by the occasional treat. This yellow magic potion is just the thing!

Ingredients for two glasses:

2 teaspoons brown sugar

½ lime

some mint

1 ¼ cups ginger ale

1 cup passion fruit juice

ice cubes

Preparation:

Cut the lime into chunks and divide them into two glasses. Put a teaspoon of brown sugar in each and crush both with a pestle. Then add a few ice cubes to the glasses and fill them up with ginger ale and passion fruit juice.

Finally, add the mint to the glass, stir well and you're ready to enjoy!

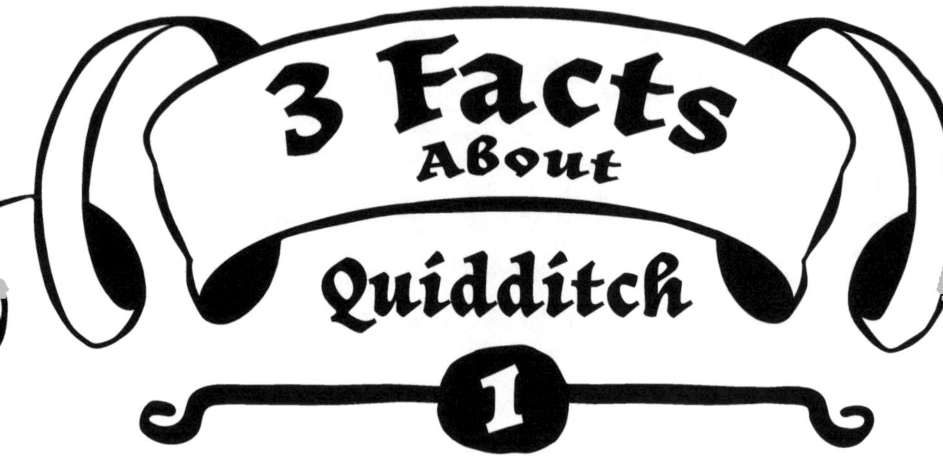

The first Quidditch World Cup in the wizarding world took place in 1473. At that time, however, only teams from Europe took part.

Minerva McGonagall was considered a gifted Quidditch player in her school days.

Probably the fastest Quidditch game was played in 1921 when seeker Roderick Plumpton caught the snitch after just 3.5 seconds.

3

The Guess Who Challenge

Take part in an exciting puzzle game in which mysteri-ous clues about a character from the *Potter* universe are gradually revealed.

When you think you have solved the mystery, write your answer on the line. Then check your answer against the solution on the next page.

Can you guess the character we are looking for with less than 10 clues?

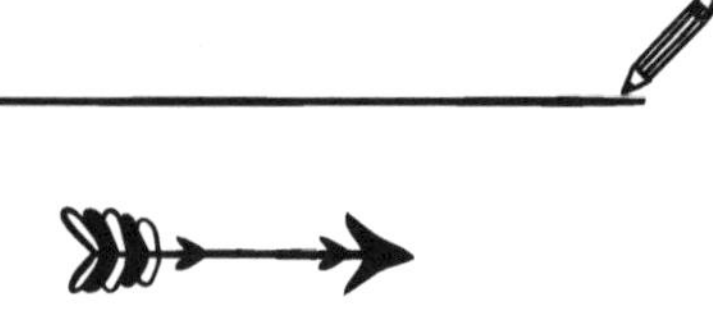

Tip: Some clues can be assigned to more than one character. Pay particular attention to those that really only apply to one character.

— **1** —

I am part of a very large family.

— **2** —

I play a major role in all seven books in the series.

— **3** —

I come from a pure-blood wizarding family.

— **4** —

I belong to the House of Gryffindor.

— **5** —

My hair has a distinctive color.

— **6** —

My pet is a bit unusual and not very reliable.

— **7** —

One of my trademarks is my old and
somewhat battered magic wand.

— **8** —

I am terrified of spiders.

— **9** —

My first encounter with Harry Potter
was on a train.

— **10** —

I once saved my friends' lives
with a game of chess.

Check your answer
on the next page.

The person we are looking for is, of course, Ron Weasley. Like many other people, Ron suffers from a severe fear of spiders — and it's not for nothing. According to J. K. Rowling, his brother Fred is responsible for this by turning Ron's childhood teddy bear into a spider. He probably wanted to teach his little brother a lesson after Ron broke Fred's broom at the age of three.

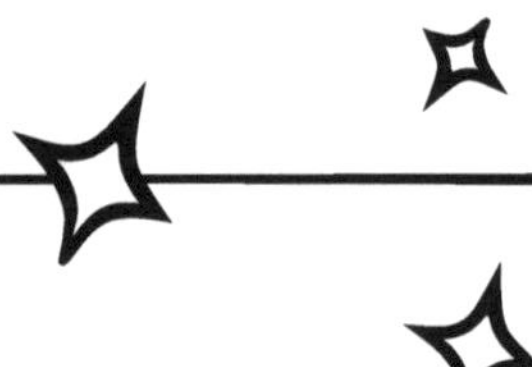

At an average reading speed, it would take a book lover around 70 hours to read the entire *Potter* series in one go.

4

Did You Know That ...

... Professor Slughorn's favorite food
is crystallized pineapple?

... the Potter family made their
fortune by selling a magic hair gel?

The Find Me Challenge

Harry's adventures take him to all sorts of places, even
the most hidden corners of the wizarding world. Can you
recognize seven magical places where he ends up? The
words you are looking for are hidden vertically, horizon-
tally, and diagonally in the word grid. Circle them!

rotate page!

A	G	K	G	N	R	O	O	N	E	F	A	T	R	O	L	L	B
L	R	B	N	M	S	I	T	O	W	E	B	N	T	A	S	D	C
L	I	H	E	I	T	F	F	A	Z	K	A	B	A	N	I	U	E
L	M	O	S	N	G	H	A	G	W	A	R	D	S	G	G	N	A
E	M	G	R	I	N	G	O	T	T	S	R	G	R	R	D	G	S
Y	G	W	W	S	D	U	N	W	S	G	R	Y	F	I	D	E	R
R	O	A	D	T	S	E	C	R	L	E	T	G	A	M	T	O	R
H	T	R	T	R	B	U	P	L	A	E	C	M	E	G	O	N	D
A	T	T	C	Y	H	A	L	L	B	U	R	R	O	W	I	S	T
R	S	S	H	L	Y	U	L	E	B	R	O	Y	S	O	L	F	S

19

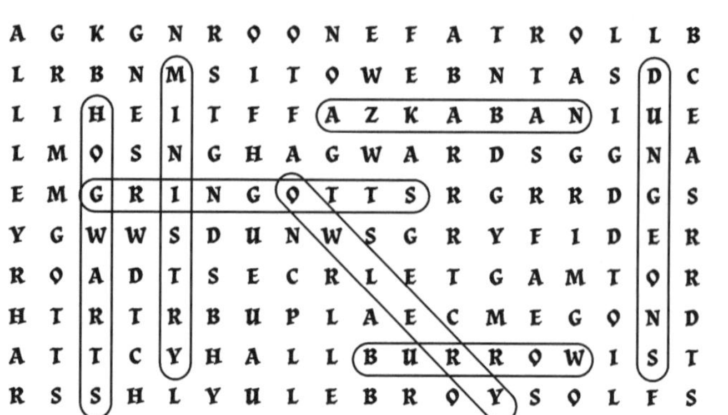

Wow of the Day

Two embroiderers who also worked for Queen Elizabeth II were involved in the production of Dumbledore's robes in the movies.

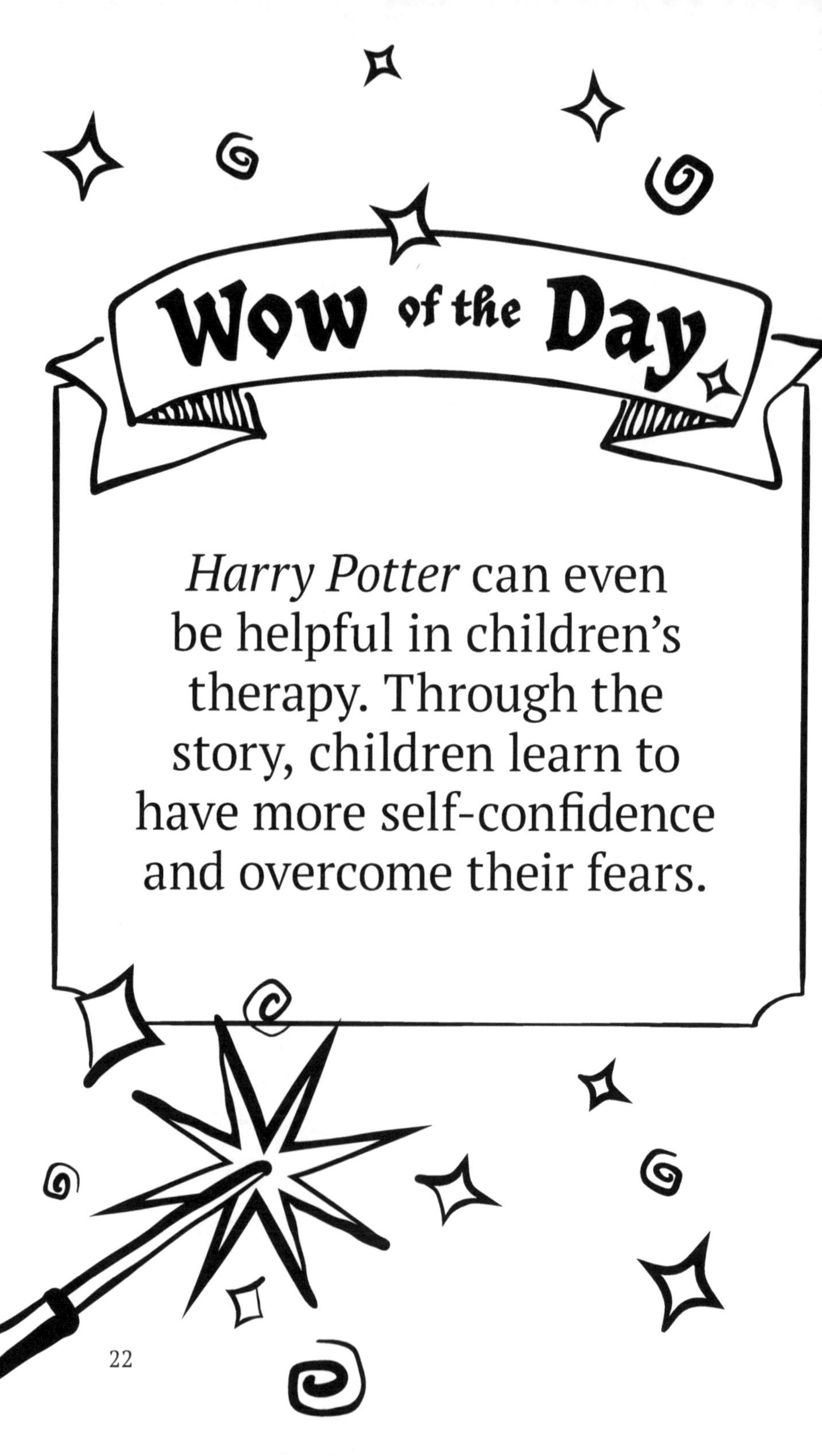

Wow of the Day

Harry Potter can even be helpful in children's therapy. Through the story, children learn to have more self-confidence and overcome their fears.

Magical Snacks

Witch Fingers

Fancy some magical cookies? Witches and wizards love to eat witch fingers. Why don't you give them a try?

Ingredients for approx. 24 pieces:

¾ cup soft butter

½ cup sugar

2 ¼ cups flour

1 egg

pinch of salt

4 tablespoons red jam

24 whole almonds

Preparation:

Mix sugar, salt, and butter in a bowl. Add the egg and stir well. Next, add the flour and mix until you have a smooth dough.

Divide the dough into 24 pieces and shape them into your witch's fingers. To do this, simply roll the dough into a thin roll. If you like, you can apply a little more pressure so that two raised areas in the roll will later become knuckles. Cut a few more lines into the joints.

Now place the fingers on a baking tray lined with baking paper. Put a small dollop of jam on the tip of each finger and place an almond on top as a fingernail. Bake them at 320 °F for about 15 minutes.

Allow the fingers to cool briefly before eating them.

There are many rumors and speculations about the Sword of Gryffindor, in particular why a wizard as talented as the founder of Hogwarts would need a sword when he already possessed a powerful wand. The explanation is rooted in the customs of his era. At the time Hogwarts was founded, sword duels were common among Muggles. It was deemed unsportsmanlike for a wizard to fight these Muggles with magical means such as a wand. As a result, Godric Gryffindor decided to master the art of sword fighting himself.

Did You Know That ...

... Remus Lupin was the first werewolf to be awarded the Order of Merlin?

... Newt Scamander considers humans to be far more evil and dangerous than any magical creature?

For a scene in *Harry Potter and the Chamber of Secrets,* Ginny actress Bonnie Wright had to lie on the cold floor for a while. To prevent her getting too cold, she put bottles of warm water under her clothes.

Sometimes it's not so easy to remember everything happening in seven books and eight movies. Here are three statements, one of which is a lie. Can you work out which statement is false without using a truth potion? Circle it. On the next page you can find out if you were right.

A Voldemort's wand contains a phoenix feather core.

B Remus Lupin has been a werewolf all his life.

C Bellatrix Lestrange is the wife of Rodolphus Lestrange.

Check your answer on the next page.

Statement B is a lie. Remus Lupin was attacked as a child by Fenrir Greyback — a werewolf — and has since turned into a wolf whenever there is a full moon.

In an early draft of *Harry Potter and the Chamber of Secrets,* the story originally involved Ron and Harry crashing the flying Ford Anglia not into the Whomping Willow, but into the Great Lake near the castle. This version would have introduced the merpeople much earlier in the series. Harry's encounter includes a description of a sea creature with a large, scaly, metallic blue-gray fish tail, and eyes that glowed gloomily and menacingly. However, J. K. Rowling decided to save a more prominent introduction of the sea creatures for a later book, which led to the alteration of this scene.

Instead of the main character Harry Potter, the story in the books begins with the appearance of his uncle Vernon Dursley. In the movies, however, it is Albus Dumbledore who is seen first.

The *Fitting* Challenge

Throughout the seven books and eight movies of the *Potter* story, Harry and his friends end up in all sorts of places. Where does none of the action take place?

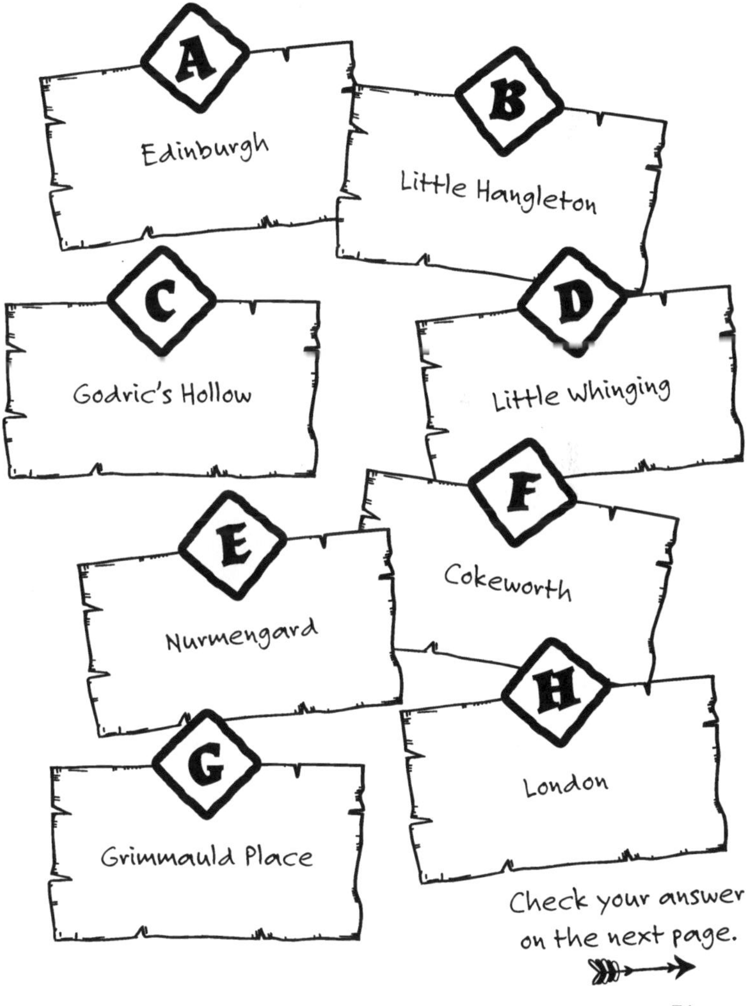

Check your answer on the next page.

If you're a real *Potter* fan and find yourself in Edinburgh, Scotland, you should definitely pay a visit to Victoria Street in the Old Town. Why? There are souvenir stores on the street that will make any fan's heart skip a beat. But that's not all: The street with its colorful houses could have been Rowling's inspiration for Diagon Alley. However, Harry and his friends never visit the town in the story (answer A).

Did You Know That ...

... before the Ministry of Magic was founded, important decisions were made by the so-called Magic Council?

... handwritten Hogwarts letters can be purchased in the House of MinaLima, the *Potter* graphic designers' store?

... 16 different versions of the Ford Anglia were used on set to bring the flying car to life?

... Harry's neighbor, Mrs. Figg, is a successful breeder of kniesel cat mongrels?

Who are we looking for here? If you have an idea of the answer, write it on the line.

— **1** —

I belong to a magical species that
often remains in the background.

— **2** —

I have a unique way of speaking.

— **3** —

I have magical abilities that are
different from those of wizards.

— **4** —

I work hard, but I'm not always treated well.

— **5** —

I am very loyal to Harry and his friends.

— **6** —

Later in the story, I work at Hogwarts.

— **7** —

I first appeared in *Harry Potter
and the Chamber of Secrets*.

— **8** —

I serve a family described in the
books as not very friendly.

— **9** —

I put my life on the line to help Harry Potter.

— **10** —

I was freed by a piece of clothing.

Check your answer
on the next page.

We are, of course, looking for the house-elf Dobby. He has accompanied Harry since his second year at Hogwarts and has been a loyal friend ever since. This is also reflected in his words. Both the first and the last words uttered by Dobby in the movies are: "Harry Potter".

Wow of the Day

In the books, Harry's story begins on a Tuesday. However, November 1, 1981, was actually a Sunday.

Before Voldemort set about turning the world of magic completely upside down, he wanted to become a teacher. However, Hogwarts twice rejected his application to become a professor of Defense Against the Dark Arts.

The When Was It Challenge

It's not easy to keep track of everything. Have you read the *Potter* books more than once? Watched the movies repeatedly? If so, this will not be a difficult task for you, and you will manage to assign the events to the correct part of the *Potter* series. Write the number of the volume or movie in which the respective event first occurs in the box. On the next page you can check whether your knowledge of magic is really good enough.

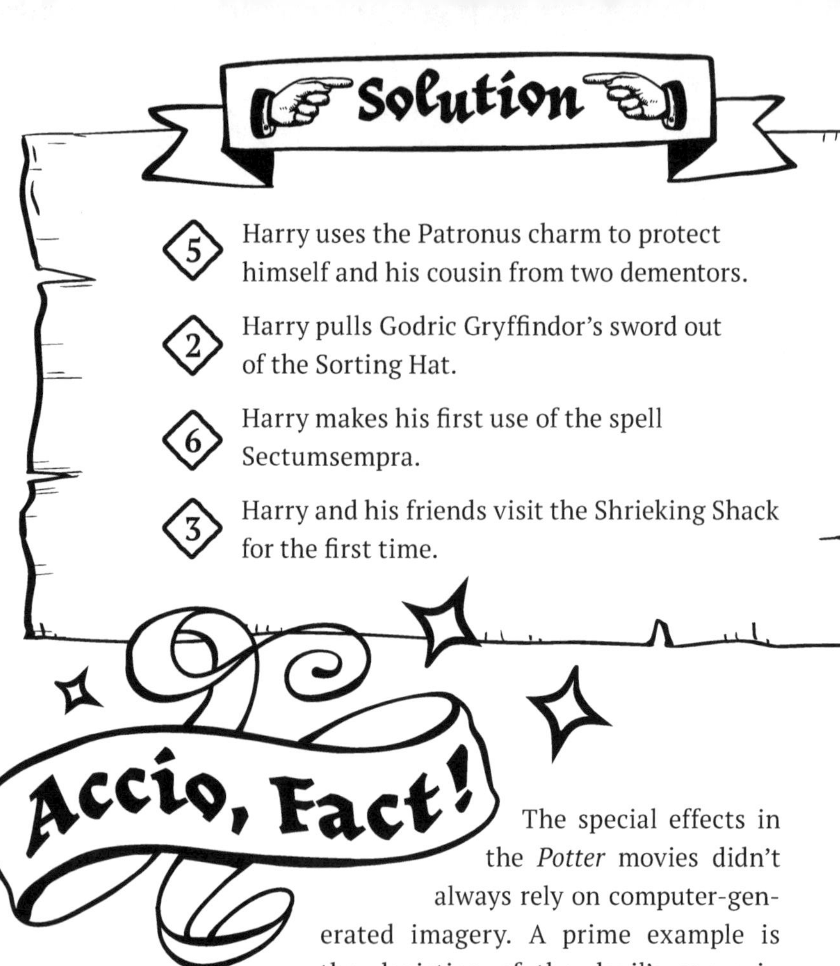

5 Harry uses the Patronus charm to protect himself and his cousin from two dementors.

2 Harry pulls Godric Gryffindor's sword out of the Sorting Hat.

6 Harry makes his first use of the spell Sectumsempra.

3 Harry and his friends visit the Shrieking Shack for the first time.

The special effects in the *Potter* movies didn't always rely on computer-generated imagery. A prime example is the depiction of the devil's snare in *Harry Potter and the Sorcerer's Stone*. To create the illusion of the plant moving independently, artificial tentacles were manipulated with strings. The actors were initially wrapped in these tentacles, which were then gradually pulled away by the strings. The final effect was achieved by playing the footage backwards, making it appear as if the plant was actively wrapping itself around them.

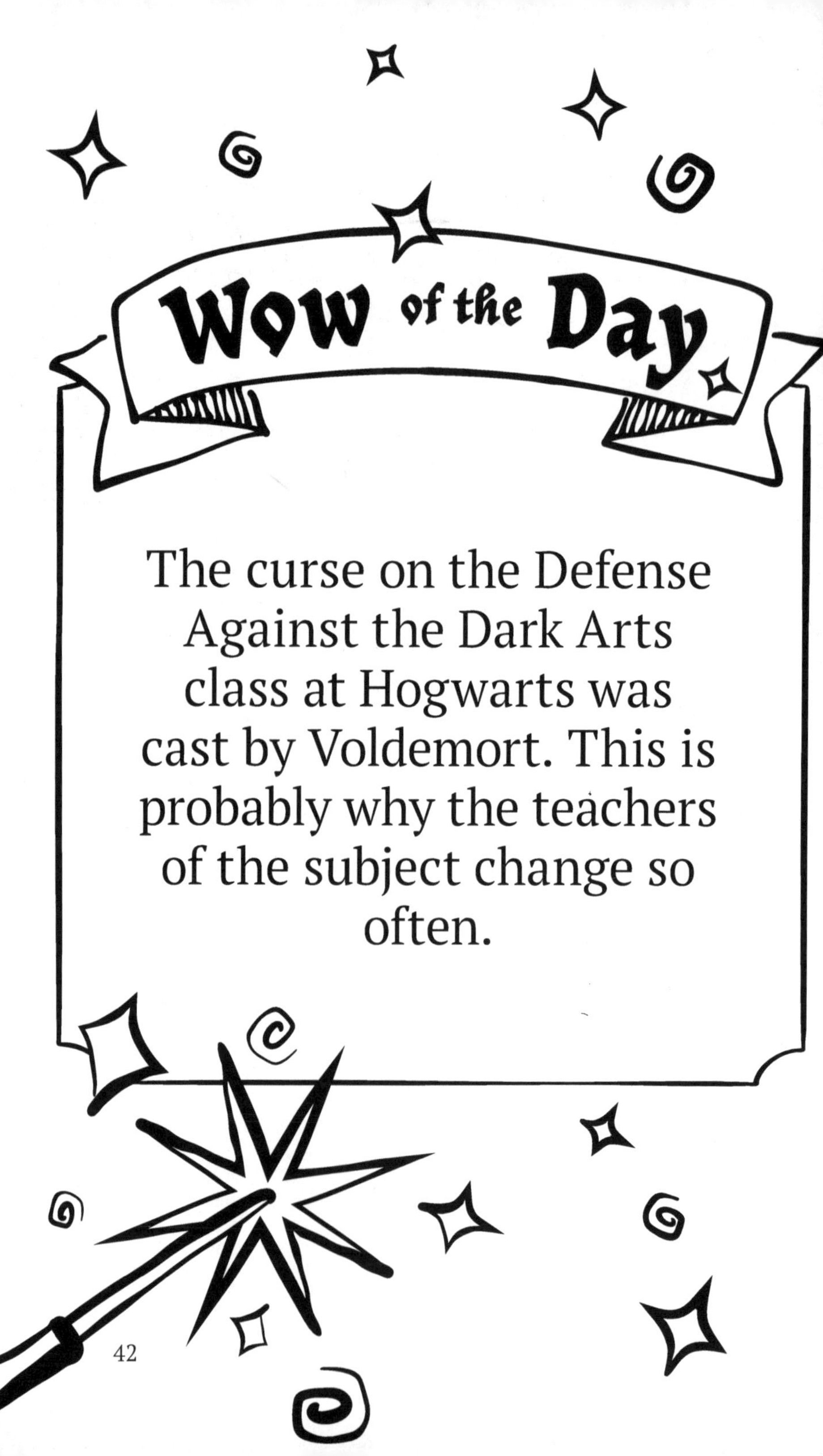

The curse on the Defense Against the Dark Arts class at Hogwarts was cast by Voldemort. This is probably why the teachers of the subject change so often.

Magic Potions

House Drink of the Red House

The lions from Gryffindor are brave and proud. But they also like to relax with a cool refreshment and enjoy life.

Ingredients for two large glasses:

2 cups water

3 bags of fruit tea

½ cup juice (such as orange, apple or passion fruit juice)

½ orange (sliced)

some mint

ice cubes

Preparation:

Bring the water to boil in a saucepan, then remove from the heat. Add the tea bags, mint, orange slices and juice and stir everything well. Leave the tea to steep for about five minutes, then remove the mint leaves and tea bags.

Allow the tea to cool well and then pour it into glasses with a few ice cubes. If you like, you can garnish the glasses with some mint and orange slices.

Enjoy the taste!

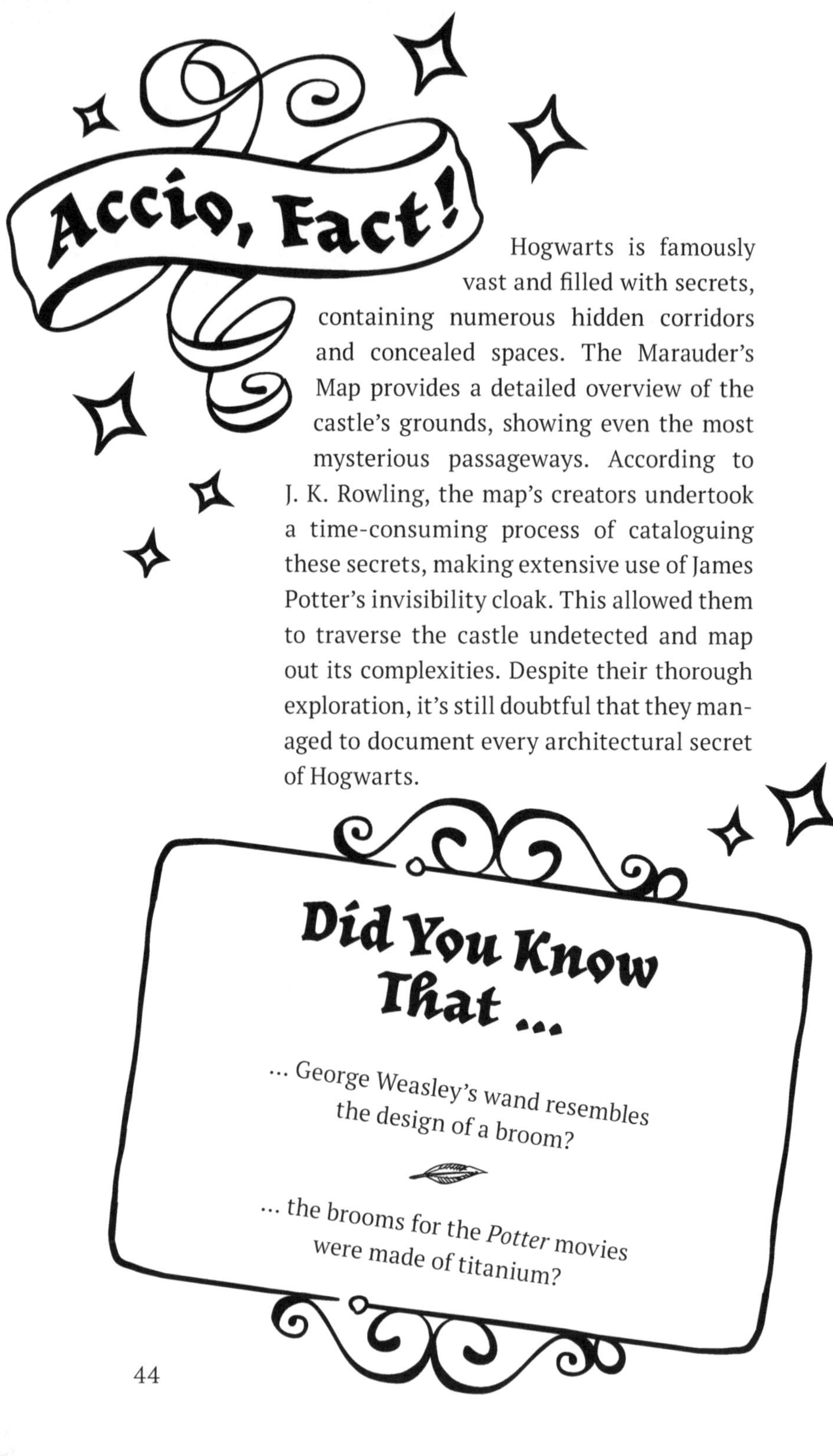

Hogwarts is famously vast and filled with secrets, containing numerous hidden corridors and concealed spaces. The Marauder's Map provides a detailed overview of the castle's grounds, showing even the most mysterious passageways. According to J. K. Rowling, the map's creators undertook a time-consuming process of cataloguing these secrets, making extensive use of James Potter's invisibility cloak. This allowed them to traverse the castle undetected and map out its complexities. Despite their thorough exploration, it's still doubtful that they managed to document every architectural secret of Hogwarts.

Did You Know That ...

… George Weasley's wand resembles the design of a broom?

… the brooms for the *Potter* movies were made of titanium?

As a child, Harry is brought to the Dursleys on a flying motorcycle. He leaves them in the same way in the final volume.

To Muggle eyes, most magical objects look quite ordinary. They have no idea of the hidden power within. Can you recognize all seven magical items in the word grid?

howler

amulet

snitch

bludger

pensieve

cauldron

parchment

C A U L T A R E P A P A R H R C S H
E P L V D O P B Y B E H L O P H U I
A C E T T C A U L D R O N G E A R D
M L D N P A R C K M B W F S N M E D
U A H A S N I T C H R L F M C A L E
L S S E C I T B E G T E U B R L I T
E T H I Q U E D D I T R O D U E F T
T S P R I N L V Q B R O M R G T Z R
A M P A R C H M E N T Q U A T E H E
R E T D U N G A O M D R A N G U R A

C A U L T A R E P A P A R H R C S H
E P L V D O P B Y B E H L O P H U I
A C E T T C A U L D R O N G E A R D
M L D N P A R C K M B W F S N M E D
U A H A S N I T C H R L F M C A L E
L S S E C I T B E G T E U B R L I T
E T H I Q U E D D I T R O D U E F T
T S P R I N L V Q B R O M R G T Z R
A M P A R C H M E N T Q U A T E H E
R E T D U N G A O M D R A N G U R A

Did You Know That ...

... the video game *Minecraft* features a fan-built version of the wizarding world, including Hogwarts and Diagon Alley?

... the Sorting Hat was first created as a puppet before the digital version was developed for the movie?

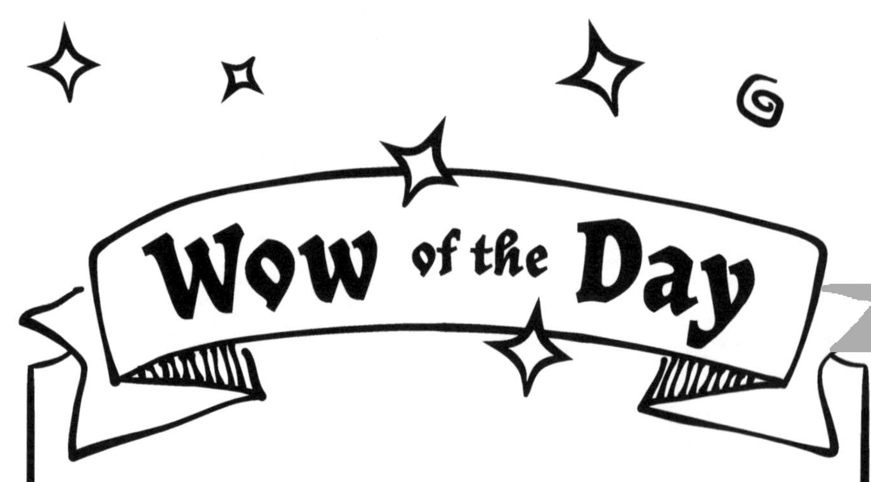

Rowling needed a lot of patience to get the first *Potter* book published. A whole year passed before a publisher finally expressed interest in her manuscript about the young wizard.

... *Harry Potter* made boarding schools popular again in the UK?

... Severus Snape's clothes have changed very little over the course of the movies?

The Veritas Challenge

Again, the question is: truth or lie? Circle the false statement.

A The Dark Mark that every Death Eater bears also shows a snake.

B Floo Powder can be used to cure minor injuries.

C Ireland won the 1994 Quidditch World Cup, which Harry visits.

Check your answer on the next page.

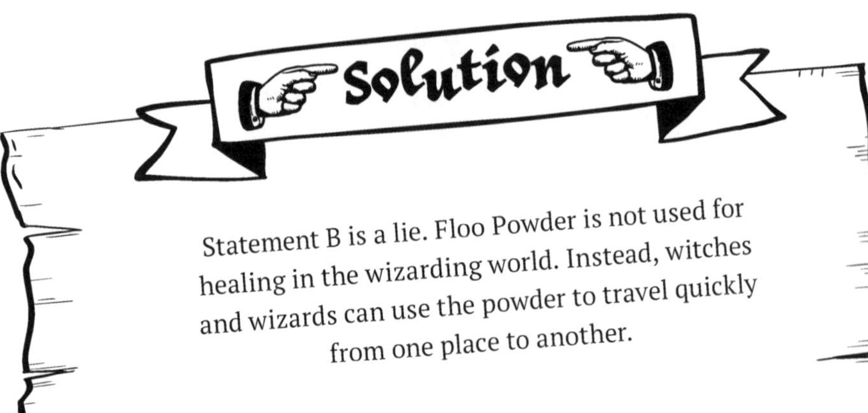

Statement B is a lie. Floo Powder is not used for healing in the wizarding world. Instead, witches and wizards can use the powder to travel quickly from one place to another.

Ian Hart, who played Quirrell in the first *Harry Potter* movie, was unfamiliar with the story when he landed the role of the Defense Against the Dark Arts teacher. To catch up, he visited a bookstore to purchase the first book of the series, but was mistakenly given the second book, *Harry Potter and the Chamber of Secrets*. As he read it, Hart was puzzled by the seeming insignificance of his role, as Quirrell didn't appear in that book at all. Only later did he realize that he had actually secured a substantial role as the antagonist in the first movie.

13

Did You Know That ...

... Ron actor Rupert Grint auditioned
for his role with a rap video?

... Harry's grandparents never got to know their
grandson because dragon pox carried
them off before Harry was born.

The Guess Who Challenge

Go through the clues one by one. If you think you have
guessed the character we are looking for, write it on the
line.

I belong to an old and well-known
family of wizards.

My appearance is defined by a time
of hard trials.

My name is also that of a constellation.

My loyalty to my friends is unshakeable.

My death is tragic and happens in a fight.

I can transform into a certain animal.

At first, many people thought I
was a dangerous criminal.

My family home is an important meeting
place for the Order of the Phoenix.

My first appearance is in *Harry Potter
and the Prisoner of Azkaban*.

I am the godfather of one of the main characters.

Check your answer
on the next page.

The wizard you are looking for is, of course, Sirius Black. In one of Rowling's notes, there was an entry about Sirius' death happening in a different way. The early draft had Sirius choose death over emptiness at the hands of a dementor, implying that he ended his life willingly. Luckily, Rowling decided not to use this idea in the end.

Wow of the Day

The ghost, known to *Potter* fans as Moaning Myrtle, was initially thought to be called "Wailing Wanda".

14

Fluffy the three-headed dog seems truly unique. Even his three heads have their very own personalities. One is always tired, one is particularly clever, and the third is extremely alert.

Magical Snacks

Troll Feet

Admittedly: Trolls are not always considered particularly desirable. But when it comes to this recipe for troll feet, nobody can get enough of them!

Ingredients for about 15 pieces:

¼ cup soft butter

2 cups flour

pinch of salt

¼ cup sour cream

¼ cup + a little more grated cheese

1 egg yolk

1 tablespoon milk

dried herbs

Preparation:

To make the dough, mix together the butter, flour, salt, sour cream, and ¼ cup of the grated cheese. Leave the dough to rest in the fridge for about 30 minutes.

Remove from the fridge and roll out to ¼ inch thick. Then use a cookie cutter to cut out feet and place them on a baking tray lined with baking paper.

Next, mix the egg yolk with the milk and brush the mixture over each foot. Then add some grated cheese and a few dried herbs and bake the troll feet at 350 °F for about eight minutes.

... the repair spell Reparo should not be used on living creatures?

... the Potters and the Grangers were to be neighbors in early considerations?

In the sixth *Harry Potter* movie, a ring appears that is a Horcrux. Although the movie's prop department knew that the ring contained a stone, they were initially unaware that it was the Resurrection Stone. Luckily, this detail was clarified in the final *Harry Potter* book, published before the sixth movie. This timely revelation allowed the prop-makers to adjust the design of the ring to reflect its significance.

15

No fewer than 16,000 children applied for the role of Harry Potter.

Potions can prove extremely useful in certain situations. However, it is important to always have the right potion at hand. Mixing them up can have fatal consequences.

The three true love potions can be found on the next page. They are characterized by the fact that their hearts are not broken.

Ready? Then you have two minutes to find the three potions we are looking for on the next page. Let's go!

Have you found all the love potions in time? Then you can make a wish. With a little magic, it might just come true ...

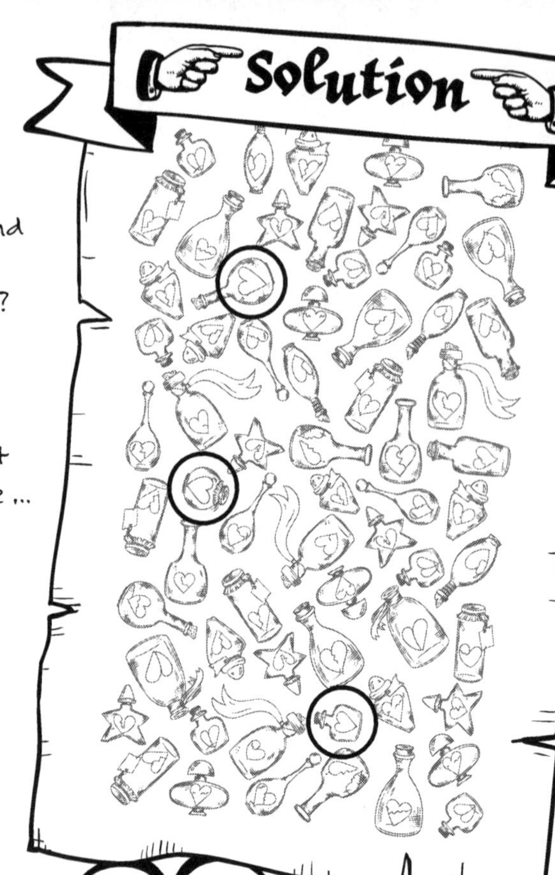

Did You Know That ...

... house-elf Kreacher wasn't supposed to appear in the fifth movie of the *Potter* series?

... about 17,000 wand boxes were made for Ollivander's store for the first *Potter* movie?

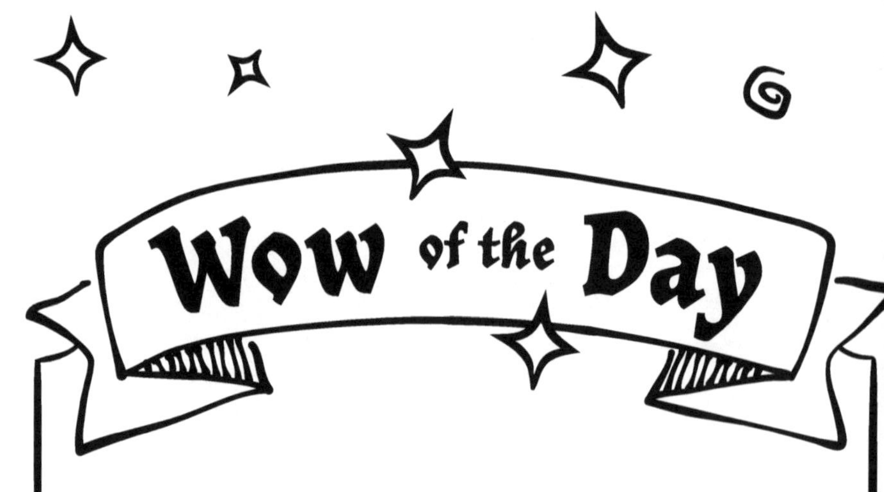

Harry Potter has even made it into the schools of British Muggles, who have had to compare the books with works by Charles Dickens or William Shakespeare as part of the curriculum.

The Fitting Challenge

Witches and wizards can buy all kinds of things on magical shopping streets like Diagon Alley. But even in the wizarding world, some items cannot be found. Can you guess which of the items below does not exist in the world of *Harry Potter*?

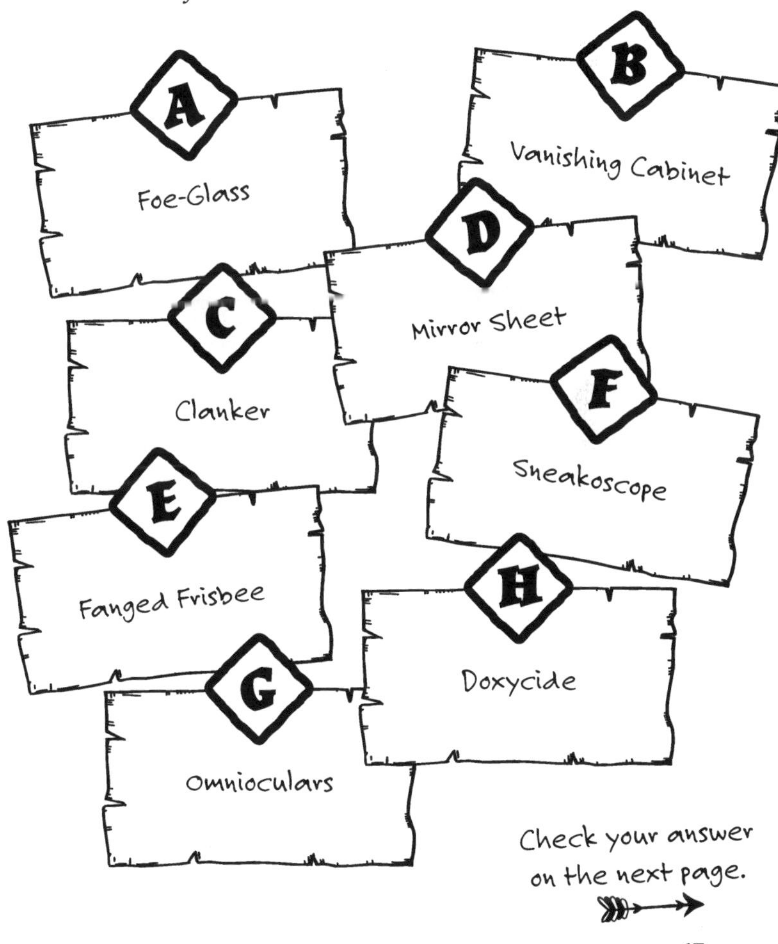

Check your answer on the next page.

In addition to the textbooks, cauldrons and other utensils needed for lessons at Hogwarts, there are all sorts of things to discover in Diagon Alley and the other magical shopping streets. There is even an ice-cream parlor. Its owner, Florean Fortsecue, was originally intended to play a more significant role in the plot of *Harry Potter*. In the end, however, Rowling decided against it. Even though the wizarding world is full of curious objects, you will never find a Mirror Sheet in Diagon Alley (answer D).

Did You Know That ...

... the largest *Harry Potter Lego* set is a 6,000-piece replica of Hogwarts Castle?

... in his school days, Gilderoy Lockhart spent Valentine's Day writing himself 800 Valentine's cards?

According to Hermione,
it is essential to maintain
eye contact when casting
a curse if it is to be
effective.

Go through the clues one by one. If you think you know
the answer, write it on the line.

____

I am a creature from the world of magic.

I've also been heard of in the Muggle world.

I was hatched from an egg.

I am closely associated with an ancient
legend and a certain house at Hogwarts.

My hiding place has not been dis-
covered for centuries.

I speak a language that only a
few wizards know.

My gaze can be deadly.

I was abandoned by one of the
founders of Hogwarts.

A dark wizard plays an important
part in my story.

I live in a hidden chamber.

Check your answer
on the next page.

The creature described is the basilisk. When *Harry Potter and the Chamber of Secrets* was being filmed, neither the audience nor the filmmakers had any idea what a major role it was going to play. The fact that Harry destroys Tom Riddle's diary with a basilisk fang, of all things, is extremely important. At the time, however, J. K. Rowling had not yet revealed any information about the Horcruxes, which in retrospect makes this scene a significant moment in the history of the books and movies.

... the actors in the *Potter* movies had to hand in their wands back after each shoot.

... the Burrow is destroyed in the sixth movie of the *Potter* series, but remains intact in the book?

18

The motto of Hogwarts School of Witchcraft and Wizardry is "Draco dormiens nunquam titillandus". This Latin phrase translates to "never tickle a sleeping dragon", and serves as a whimsical yet wise warning to students and staff alike.

Magic Potions

House Drink of the Green House

Fresh and slightly sour, this is the drink of choice for the ambitious snakes of the green house.

Ingredients for two glasses:

1 lime

2 teaspoons brown sugar

some mint

1 ¼ cups apple juice

1 cup sparkling water

¼ teaspoon lemon lime drink mix powder

ice cubes

a slice of green apple

Preparation:

Cut the lime in half and then into chunks. Now divide them into the glasses together with a teaspoon of sugar. Add a few mint leaves to each glass and crush everything.

Now add lemon lime drink mix powder to each glass and fill them with apple juice and water. Finally, drop a slice of apple into the glasses for decoration.

That's it!

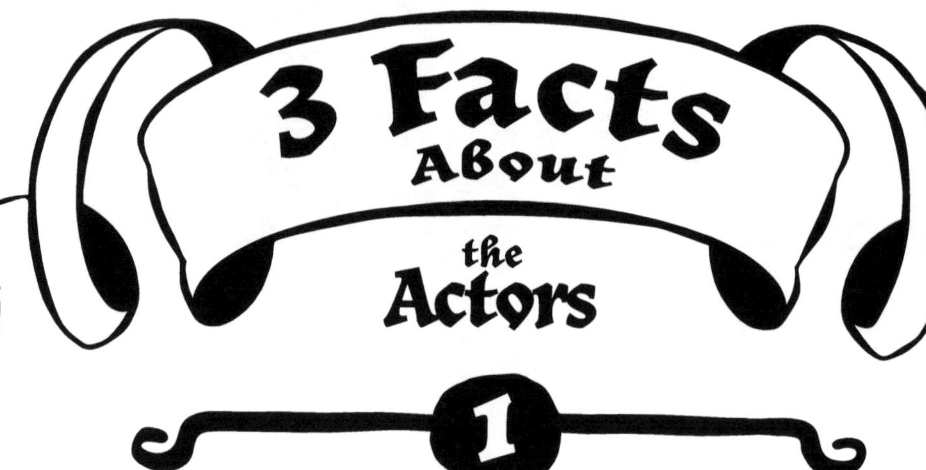

1

Lucius actor Jason Isaacs found the replica of Fawkes the phoenix so lifelike that he thought it was a real bird on set.

2

Emma Watson not only memorized the lines for her role as Hermione, but also some of her colleagues Rupert Grint and Daniel Radcliffe.

3

Harry actor Daniel Radcliffe had to shave his legs for the scene in the second movie, in which Harry frees Dobby through one of his socks.

19

The so-called logline describes the plot of a story in a single sentence. For *Harry Potter* it reads: A boy goes to a wizarding school.

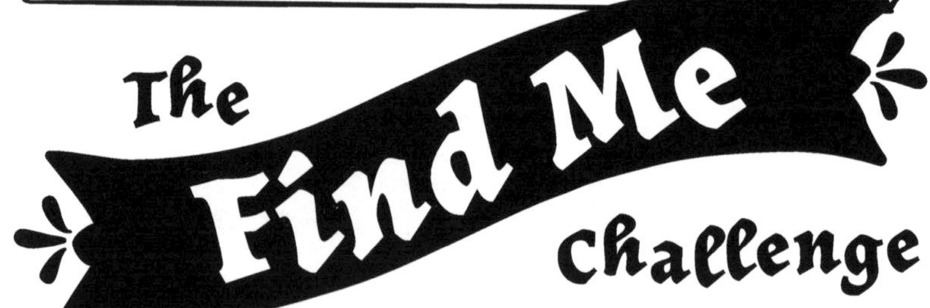

During his time at school, Harry meets some great witches and wizards. Some of them even teach at Hogwarts. Can you find all seven professors hidden in the word grid?

Lupin

Sprout

Flitwick

Umbridge

Lockhart

Quirrell

Moody

D	U	B	M	D	O	R	E	F	A	D	G	E	R	O	N	P	E
G	D	Y	F	L	R	E	U	G	O	O	B	A	Q	S	K	L	P
A	O	L	U	P	I	N	H	R	E	C	M	S	U	T	A	O	H
S	B	Q	O	M	A	P	R	A	X	U	S	H	I	E	P	C	O
S	L	U	E	O	B	O	W	B	G	R	S	P	R	S	R	K	E
U	Y	Y	M	T	T	R	E	B	P	R	D	E	R	R	A	H	N
S	Q	T	O	X	F	L	I	T	W	I	C	K	E	O	M	A	I
Q	U	I	O	R	E	S	R	D	I	E	Q	D	L	N	U	R	Z
T	R	A	D	L	W	A	N	E	G	E	U	T	L	A	M	T	E
A	H	W	Y	O	T	L	O	O	D	E	Y	T	R	O	L	L	D

Accio, Fact!

Witches and wizards commonly use brooms for flying, although their magical abilities could probably be used to transform more comfortable objects, such as armchairs into flying vehicles. The primary reason they stick with brooms isn't the convenience of the cleaning tool itself, but rather its inconspicuousness and practicality. Brooms don't look suspicious to Muggles and are more portable than bulky items like sofas, making them a practical choice for magical travel.

20

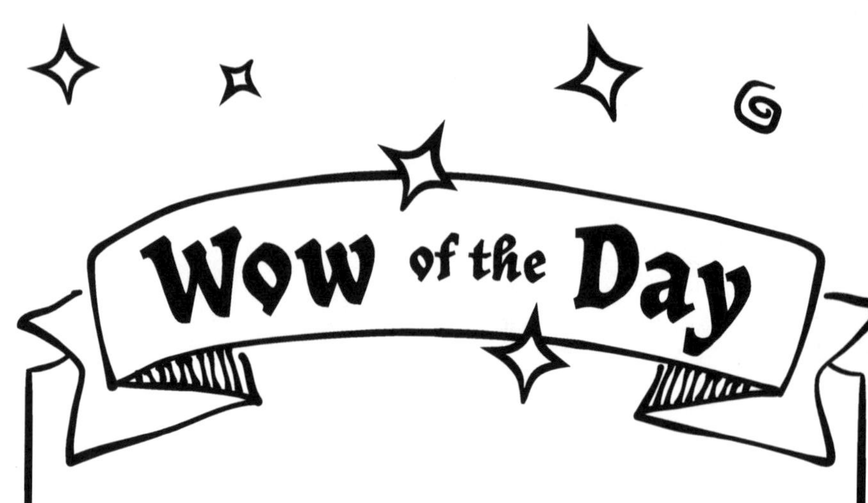

Ron actor Rupert Grint is also afraid of spiders in real life and even had to avert his eyes during the spider scenes at the movie premiere of *Harry Potter and the Chamber of Secrets.*

The When Was It Challenge

Match the events to the correct book/movie. As usual, you will find the solution on the next page.

- Rita Kimmkorn publishes a scandalous article about Harry and Hermione.

- Harry and Cho Chang have their first date in the village of Hogsmeade.

- Harry attends a Christmas dinner at Professor Slughorn's house.

- Harry discovers that he is a Parselmouth.

- Harry buys Omnioculars for himself and his friends.

④ Rita Kimmkorn publishes a scandalous article about Harry and Hermione.

⑤ Harry and Cho Chang have their first date in the village of Hogsmeade.

⑥ Harry attends a Christmas dinner at Professor Slughorn's house.

② Harry discovers that he is a Parselmouth.

④ Harry buys Omnioculars for himself and his friends.

Accio, Fact!

The Weasley family's residence, known as the Burrow, is portrayed in the movies as an exceptionally warm and welcoming home, albeit a slightly chaotic one. This is not surprising given the size of the family. What stands out most is the house's seemingly crooked structure. The set designers intentionally achieved this by removing various beams and adjusting some of the walls, aiming to give the house a distinctive look that suited the family living in it. Indeed, they succeeded in their mission.

21

J. K. Rowling spent a year teaching English in Portugal, where she found the inspiration for the Hogwarts students' capes. These cloaks are influenced by the clothing worn by Portuguese university students.

Did You Know That ...

... the design of the phoenix Fawkes
is based on a sea eagle?

... Ron's father is not an only child,
but has two brothers?

The Veritas Challenge

Can you recognize the false statement from these three?
Circle it.

A The anniversary of Severus Snape's death
is May 2, 1998.

B Sirius Black has the ability to transform
into a large dog.

C J. K. Rowling and Voldemort share the
same birthday.

Check your answer
on the next page.

Statement C is a lie. J. K. Rowling shares her birthday with Harry Potter. Both were born on July 31.

On the set of *Harry Potter and the Goblet of Fire*, all the actors had to take special dance lessons to prepare for the Yule Ball scene, except Daniel Radcliffe. Due to his busy filming schedule, he simply couldn't spare the time for dance training. While his co-stars practiced for about three weeks, Radcliffe had just four days to learn the dance moves. When shooting the dance scene, he was strategically filmed from the hips up to ensure that his feet were never shown. This clever camera work helped hide any missteps and kept his dance skills, or lack thereof, from detracting from the scene.

22

The Great Lake's Kraken

All kinds of magical creatures live in the depths of the Great Lake. But few are as tasty as these kraken muffins!

Ingredients for about 12 muffins:

For the batter:

4 eggs

¾ cup sugar

pinch of salt

½ cup sunflower oil

1 ¾ cups flour

3 teaspoons baking powder

½ cup sparkling water

Preparation:

Mix all the batter ingredients in a large bowl until smooth. Pour the mixture into a muffin tin lined with paper cases and bake at 320 °F for about 25 minutes.

When the muffins are ready, take them out of the oven and leave them to cool thoroughly. Then it's time to decorate.

Mix the juice of one lemon with the icing sugar and stir well. Then add some blue food coloring and spread the icing over the muffins — this will be the water for your krakens.

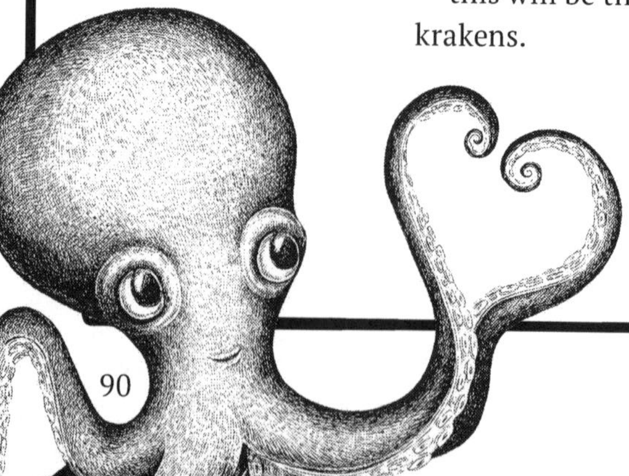

For decoration:

jelly babies (12 round ones and some in the shape of worms)

candy eyes

1 lemon

1 ½ cups icing sugar

blue food coloring

For the krakens themselves, spread some jelly worms on the muffins for tentacles and place a round fruit gum on top as a body. You can then decorate this with the candy eyes.

Your yummy-looking krakens are ready!

Did You Know That ...

... Rowling is the first living author to have an exhibition dedicated to her at the British Library?

... according to the Marauder's map, Hogwarts has a repair shop for the Monster Book of Monsters?

The *Potter* books were only published in digital form in 2011, which is comparatively late. Before that, J. K. Rowling had refused to publish the stories about the young wizard as e-books.

23

If you are as skilled at magic as Grindelwald, Dumbledore or Voldemort, you may even become invisible without a cloak of invisibility.

Once again, we are looking for a well-known character. If you think you know it, write the name on the line.

1

I wear half-moon spectacles.

2

I am known for my long silver hair and my beard.

3

In my youth, I was friends with a dark wizard.

4

I was involved in the discovery of
the 12 uses of dragon's blood.

5

I love sweets, especially sherbet lemons.

6

My magic wand hides a well-kept secret.

7

My death is a turning point in the story.

8

I am a founding member and leader
of the Order of the Phoenix.

9

I am one of the wisest and most powerful characters in the series.

10

I am a headmaster of Hogwarts.

Check your answer
on the next page.

This, of course, is Professor Albus Dumbledore. The headmaster of Hogwarts is a man of few words. But he is by no means mute. If you read the Italian version of the *Potter* books, you might get the impression that he is. There, Professor Dumbledore is translated as "Professor Silente", meaning "Professor Silent". This could be due to the similarity between the English part of the word "dumb" (which can also mean "mute") and the name Dumbledore. However, the name Dumbledore actually comes from the Old English word for "bumblebee".

Did You Know That ...

... Quidditch might be such a violent sport because Rowling invented it after a fight with her partner?

... the intro to the *Potter* movies grows darker with each instalment?

24

In the end credits of *Harry Potter and the Prisoner of Azkaban,* the Marauder's Map shows the activities within Hogwarts. Hagrid's footprints are particularly striking. They are significantly larger than those of the students and teachers. Of course, this is completely intentional. After all, Hagrid is a half-giant.

Did You Know That ...

... Muggles only see ruins when they get too close to Hogwarts due to a protection spell?

... the color green often symbolizes black magic?

Accio, Fact! Typically, J. K. Rowling did not let the movie adaptations influence her writing. However, there were a few exceptions. One such instance occurred in *Harry Potter and the Order of the Phoenix*. During a scene in the Forbidden Forest, Hermione and her friends lure Professor Umbridge to a giant who grabs the unpopular headmistress. In creating this scene, Rowling considered how it would appear on screen and how filmmakers might bring it to life. She allowed these visual considerations to influence her writing to some extent for this particular passage.

Magic Potions

House Drink of the Blue House

The eagles of the blue house have certainly put a lot of their creativity and intelligence into this recipe. Will you like it as much as they do?

Ingredients for two glasses:

½ cup sparkling water

2 teaspoons lemon juice

2 cups lemonade

2 lemon slices

some blue food coloring

ice cubes

Preparation:

Pour the lemon juice and a little blue food coloring into the glasses and stir the mixture briefly. Fill the glasses with lemonade and water, then add a slice of lemon to each glass.

You're ready to enjoy!

25

Wow of the Day

It's not just Muggles who find Christmas trees magical, and there is certainly something magical about the trees at Hogwarts. In the movie *Harry Potter and the Sorcerer's Stone*, little witches fly around the treetops.

The Magical Quiz for the Whole Family

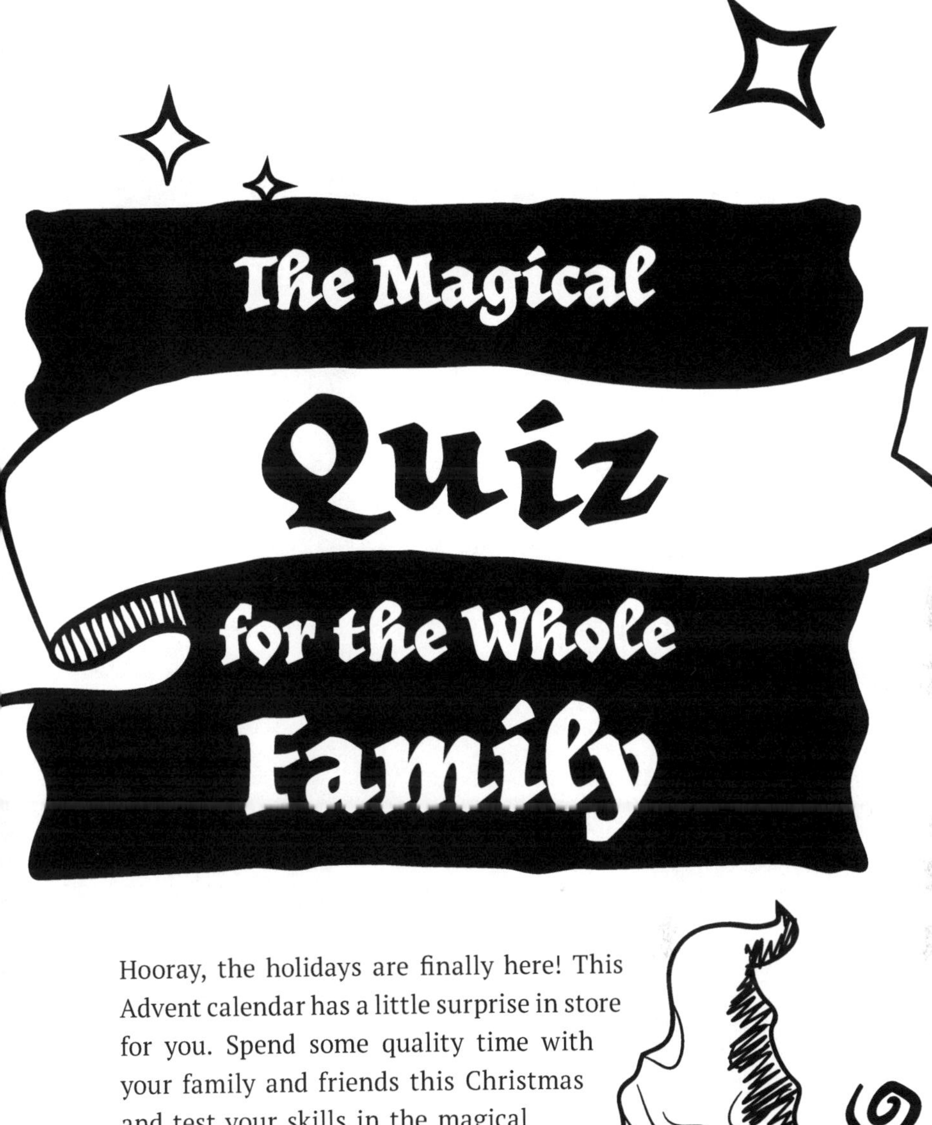

Hooray, the holidays are finally here! This Advent calendar has a little surprise in store for you. Spend some quality time with your family and friends this Christmas and test your skills in the magical quiz.

Rules of the Game

The rules are simple: Cut out the game sheets on the following pages (p. 106 and p. 107) and then cut out the cards on the dashed lines.

Each player receives four answer cards (A, B, C, and D). Put the wands aside for now. Now it's time to start. The youngest wizard reads out the first question, along with the four possible answers. Each player then places their answer card face down in front of them. When everyone has answered, turn the cards over at the same time. The player who read out the question now reads out the answer.

Each player who has answered correctly receives a wand.

The next player asks a question in a clockwise direction. This continues until all the questions have been asked.

The winner of the quiz is the person who has collected the most wands after 10 questions.

A	B	C	D
A	B	C	D
A	B	C	D
A	B	C	D
A	B	C	D

If you need more playing cards or wands, you can download free templates from nucleo-media.com/magical-xmas-quiz

What is the first name of Professor Sprout, the Herbology teacher?

A Pomona

B Septima

C Minerva

D Irma

Where is the secret passage to the Shrieking Shack?

A Under the Great Hall

B Under the Whomping Willow

C Under the Enchanted Well

D Behind the Unicorn Statue

Solution

Pomona Sprout (answer A), known as the Herbology teacher at Hogwarts, also takes on the role of Head of House for Hufflepuff. In the *Harry Potter* movies, she was played by actress Miriam Margolyes. In between filming, Margolyes also appeared in other projects, including the musical *Wicked,* where she — quite fittingly — took on the role of a witch.

The passage to the Shrieking Shack is hidden under the Whomping Willow on the grounds of Hogwarts (answer B). This tree was planted by Professor Dumbledore himself. Its purpose was to both hide and protect the secret entrance beneath it. Curious students were to be prevented from discovering Remus Lupin's secret. Lupin used the shack on full moon nights so that he could stay there undisturbed in his werewolf form. No one was allowed to find out, of course.

Which role did Newt Scamander actor Eddie Redmayne originally audition for?

A Ron Weasley

B Lord Voldemort

C Cedric Diggory

D Peter Pettigrew

Where does Lucius Malfoy usually keep his wand in the movies?

A In his coat pocket

B In his trouser pocket

C Up his sleeve

D In his walking stick

Eddie Redmayne, best known to many fans of the *Harry Potter* universe as Newt Scamander, originally applied for a role in *Harry Potter and the Chamber of Secrets*. At the time, he auditioned for the role of the young Lord Voldemort (answer B) but unfortunately did not get a response for the casting of the iconic antagonist.

The villain Lucius Malfoy, with his long blond hair and distinctive walking stick, is instantly recognizable in the movies. Some of the character's features were inspired by ideas from Jason Isaacs, who played the villain. Isaacs wanted to distinguish himself from his movie son Draco with his long hair, as well as to give Lucius Malfoy more of a dimension. The walking stick in which Lucius hides his wand (answer D) was also an idea of Isaacs to add elegance and sophistication to the character.

What is the name of the piece of music that plays at the beginning of every *Potter* movie and is probably the most-recognizable tune in the series?

A *Hogwarts Awaits*

B *Time for Magic*

C *Hedwig's Theme*

D *Magical Tone*

What did the movie actors actually consume when they drank the Polyjuice Potion?

A Cucumber water with chunks

B Colored yogurt

C Vegetable soup

D Diluted gruel

The film music of the *Harry Potter* series plays a crucial role and contributes significantly to the unique atmosphere of the movies. One piece that stands out in particular is *Hedwig's Theme* by John Williams (answer C). This is, of course, the well-known melody at the beginning of every *Potter* movie. Its origin is rather unusual. Williams originally composed it for the trailer of the first *Harry Potter* movie, without having seen the actual footage. Instead of a small composition for a promotional trailer, it became the most famous piece of music in the series.

Polyjuice Potion is one of the most complex and useful potions that students have to prepare at Hogwarts. A vegetable soup with chunks was used for the movies (answer C). It was then chilled to add an extra disgusting effect. The actors' reactions to the unpleasant taste of the potion were therefore authentic.

7

Which subject did Albus Dumbledore first teach?

A Transfiguration

B Charms

C Defense Against the Dark Arts

D Muggle Studies

8

Which Weasley works at Gringotts Wizarding Bank?

A Bill Weasley

B Charlie Weasley

C Percy Weasley

D George Weasley

Professor Albus Dumbledore is known as one of the greatest and most powerful wizards in the world of *Harry Potter*. However, he also started his career in humble beginnings as a teacher at Hogwarts School of Witchcraft and Wizardry. He initially taught Defense Against the Dark Arts (answer C).

Bill Weasley, one of the Weasley family's brothers, works as a curse-breaker at the wizarding bank Gringotts (answer A). Although many movie fans may be under the impression that only goblins work at Gringotts, the *Harry Potter* books prove that talented wizards can also be employed there. In the movies, Bill only really makes an appearance in *Harry Potter and the Deathly Hallows*. However, he can already be seen briefly in a family photo in *Harry Potter and the Prisoner of Azkaban*.

How long can you breathe underwater thanks to gillyweed?

 About 30 minutes

 About an hour

 About four hours

 About a day

In which *Potter* book does Dumbledore first mention Nurmengard?

 *Harry Potter and the Goblet of Fire*

 *Harry Potter and the Order of the Phoenix*

 *Harry Potter and the Half-Blood Prince*

 *Harry Potter and the Deathly Hallows*

The outstanding effects of gillyweed only last for about an hour (answer B). Anyone using the plant must therefore hurry. During this time, however, the user can breathe underwater and adapt seamlessly to the underwater world. The user develops webbing between the fingers and toes and gills on the neck. Naturally, this magical plant remains hidden from the eyes of Muggles.

Dumbledore first mentions Nurmengard in *Harry Potter and the Half-Blood Prince* (answer C). Gellert Grindelwald is also imprisoned in the legendary prison. Voldemort, in his quest for power, seeks him out in order to obtain information about the Elder Wand. However, Grindelwald remains silent about the whereabouts of the wand, even though he knows that Dumbledore possesses it, and ultimately pays for it with his life.

Ron actor Rupert Grint came up with a very special idea for which he used his earnings from the *Potter* movies: He bought himself two llamas.

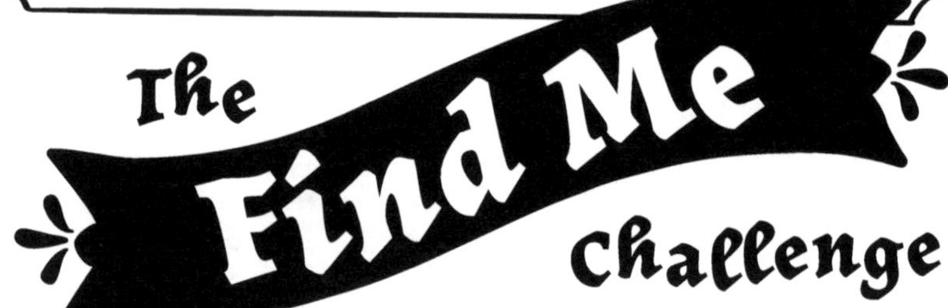

The four houses of Hogwarts are like a second family to the young witches and wizards during their time at school. Can you find seven characters who belonged to House Slytherin when they were students? We are only looking for surnames.

Parkinson

Slughorn

Zabini

Goyle

Tonks

Crabbe

Nott

L	L	U	C	I	N	K	U	Z	F	F	E	L	C	Y	S	B	S
U	K	Z	F	E	E	P	O	Q	A	K	Y	O	E	Y	K	T	F
N	V	R	A	R	E	T	A	K	A	B	I	N	D	U	A	O	L
A	A	E	E	B	V	T	K	R	A	B	I	N	R	N	M	N	O
U	C	S	R	A	I	A	B	R	K	A	D	N	C	O	M	K	H
R	H	R	S	S	L	R	I	D	D	I	L	U	I	T	R	S	S
K	O	C	A	S	L	U	G	H	O	R	N	B	K	T	E	B	A
R	N	W	I	B	R	E	R	I	N	T	T	S	P	A	R	S	E
A	G	H	Y	U	B	Q	H	E	R	M	O	G	O	Y	L	E	M
B	F	L	E	R	U	E	W	I	K	N	Y	V	O	N	G	E	L

```
L L U C I N K U Z F F E L C Y S B S
U K Z F E E P O Q A K Y O E Y K T F
N V R A R E T A K A B I N D U A O L
A A E E B V T K R A B I N R N M N O
U C S R A I A B R K A D N C O M K H
R H R S L R I D D I L U I T R S S
K O C A S L U G H O R N B K T E B A
R N W I B R E R I N T T S P A R S E
A G H Y U B Q H E R M O G O Y L E M
B F L E R U E W I K N Y V O N G E L
```

Accio, Fact!

While the sixth movie revealed that Professor Severus Snape was the enigmatic "Half-Blood Prince", it did not explore the origins of the name. However, readers of the books are provided with this backstory. It is explained that Snape's mother was a witch, while his father was a Muggle, thus making Snape a "Half-Blood". The title "Prince" comes from his mother's maiden name, Prince.

During filming, the actors were not allowed to participate in any contact sports because of the risk of injury. Instead, the cast played a few rounds of golf.

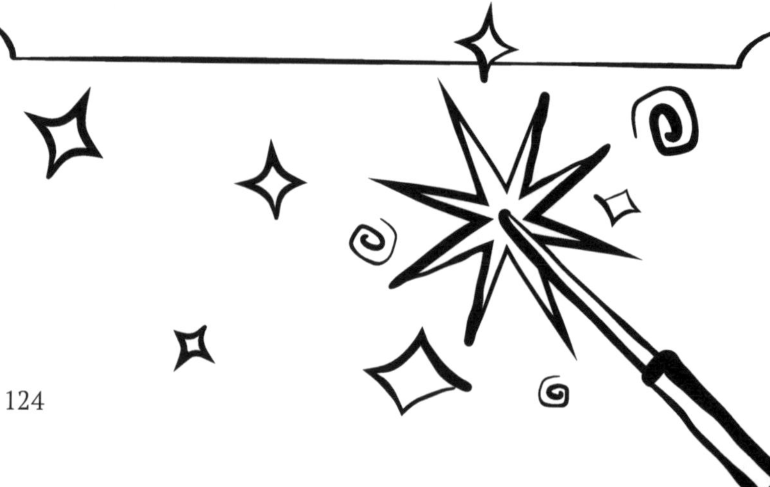

The *Fitting* Challenge

Do you have what it takes to be a real magizoologist? Can you identify which of these magical creatures doesn't actually exist in the *Potter* world?

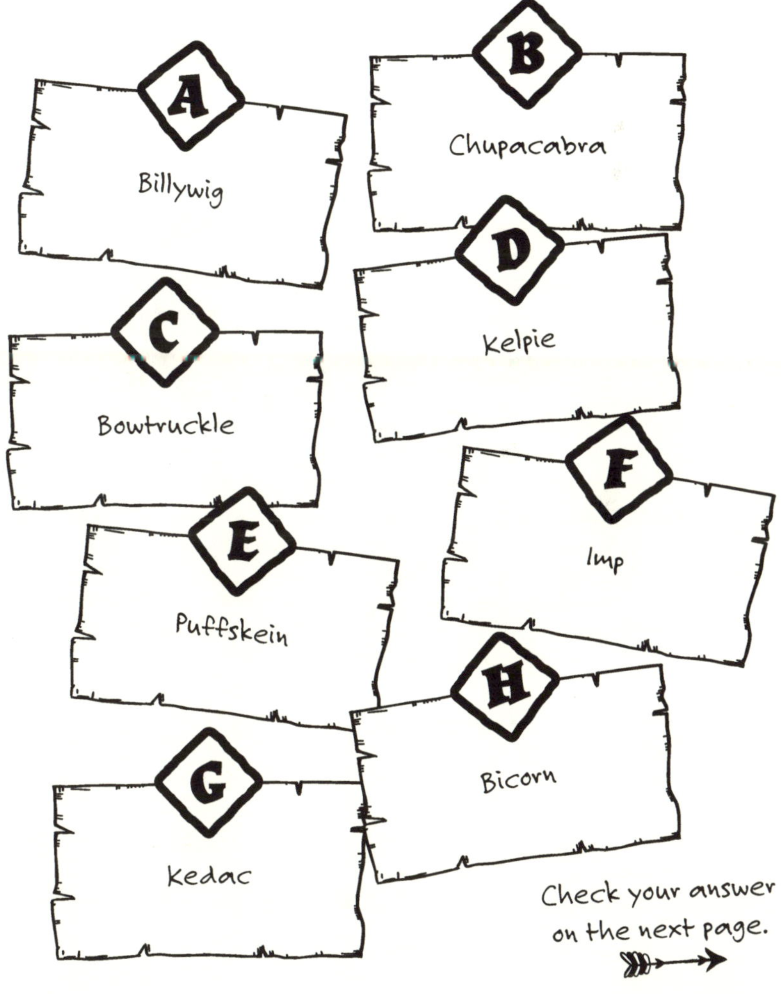

Check your answer on the next page.

St. Mungo's Hospital is the place to go for witches and wizards who have been injured due to magic. The facility has five floors, each specializing in the treatment of certain medical conditions. On the second floor are patients whose injuries have been caused by magical creatures. However, none of them have been attacked by a Kedac (answer G). These creatures do not exist.

Did You Know That ...

... before Warner Bros. acquired the film rights to *Harry Potter*, Disney was also considered a possible production studio for the movies?

... Ron actor Rupert Grint was temporarily shot at with a ball throwing machine on the set for the Quidditch scenes?

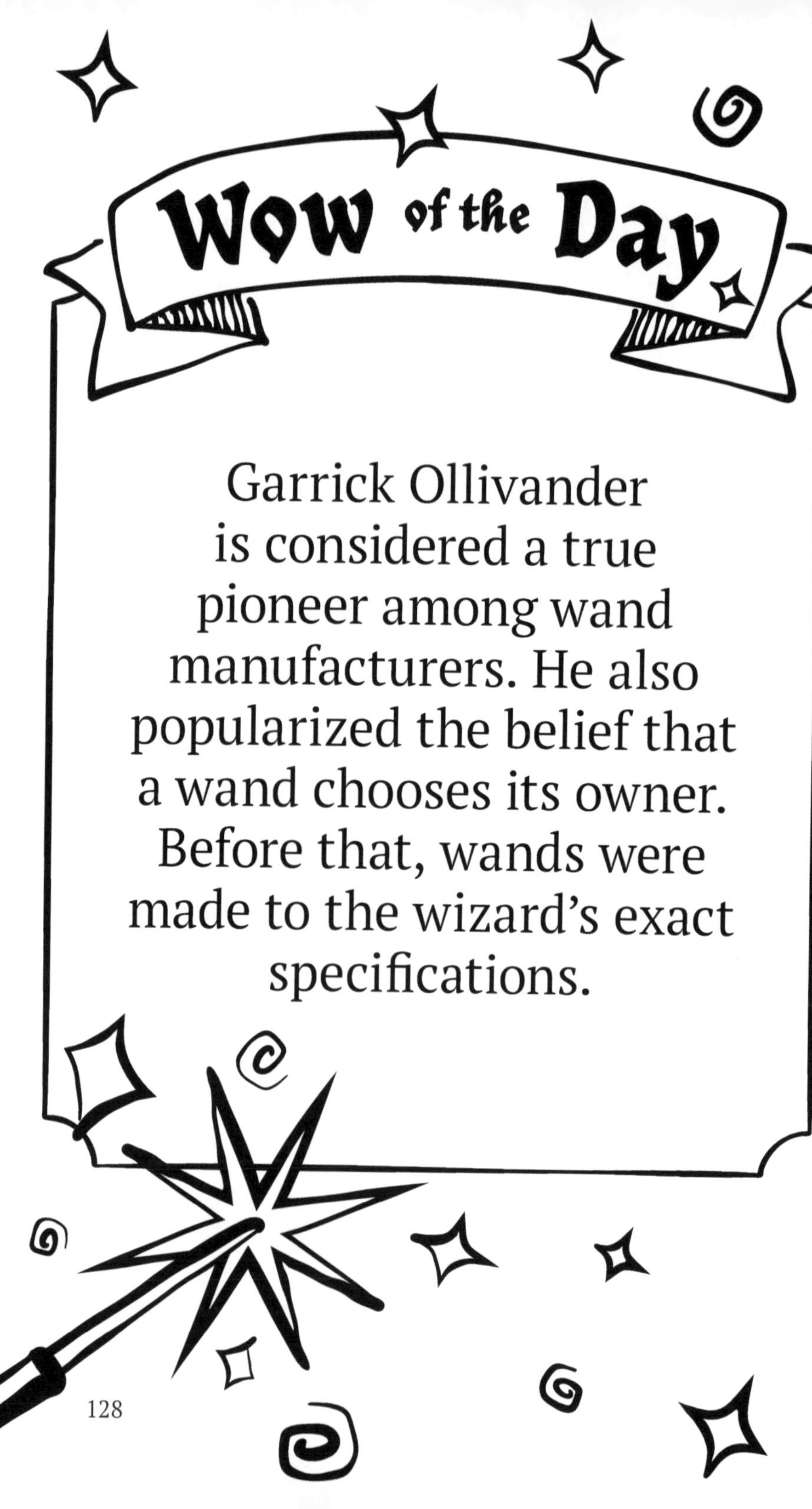

Garrick Ollivander is considered a true pioneer among wand manufacturers. He also popularized the belief that a wand chooses its owner. Before that, wands were made to the wizard's exact specifications.

Phoenix Nests

The majestic phoenixes are rarely seen in the wild, even in the magical world. However, you can easily bring their nests into your home with this recipe.

Ingredients for about 12 nests:

8 oz spaghetti

½ onion

3 egg yolks

1 cup cream

salt and pepper

½ cup Parmesan cheese

3 oz ham

Preparation:

Cook the spaghetti in water according to the instructions on the packet and then drain.

Dice the ham and onion into small cubes. Add both to the cooked spaghetti and pour the cream and egg over everything. Finally, add the Parmesan and mix well.

Pour the mixture into a muffin tin and bake at 360 °F for about 15–20 minutes.

Serve hot or cold: These phoenix nests are crispy and delicious.

Accio, Fact!

The culinary spreads at Hogwarts feasts are always exceptionally appealing, designed to make viewers eager to dive right in. However, each dish is the result of meticulous planning. The filmmakers paid a great deal of attention to detail to ensure that the food reflected the specific occasion and atmosphere of the feasts. A notable example is the abundant display of chocolate at the feast in the fourth *Potter* movie, which was used to welcome students from other schools. The choice of chocolate is intriguing; a closer look reveals that many of the chocolate creations feature three different shades: dark, milk, and white chocolate. This detail could be a subtle nod to the Triwizard Tournament featured in the movie, where the number three is a major theme.

Did You Know That ...

... most young witches and wizards are taught at home before they go to school?

... the suit Ron wears to the Yule Ball in the movie is partly made from an old carpet?

29

To minimize reflections
on the movie set as
much as possible, Harry's
glasses in most scenes
had no lenses.

Go through the clues one by one. If you think you have
guessed the character we are looking for, write it on the
line.

I am a member of the Order
of the Phoenix.

I am part of a large, loving
family of wizards.

I have survived an attack by one of
Lord Voldemort's followers.

I am fascinated by the non-magical world.

I drive a flying car.

I am married with several children.

One of my sons works with dragons.

I work at the Ministry of Magic.

One of my children is a close friend
of Harry Potter.

My house, the Burrow, is a safe
haven for Harry and his friends.

Check your answer
on the next page.

The person we are looking for is, of course, Arthur Weasley. The wizard is remarkable in his own right, but there is something else behind his name. In fact, some of the characters in his family have interesting parallels with the well-known legend of King Arthur. Arthur Weasley apparently shares his first name with the legendary King Arthur. Percy Weasley's name can be traced back to Percival, another character from the legend, and Ginny's full name, Ginevra, was also the name of King Arthur's wife. Even Ron can be included here: King Arthur's spear was called Rhongomyniad — Ron for short.

Did You Know That ...

... Hogwarts students need seven Lockhart books for their second-year lessons?

... there are special covers for adult *Potter* fans because the original books looked too childish for older readers?

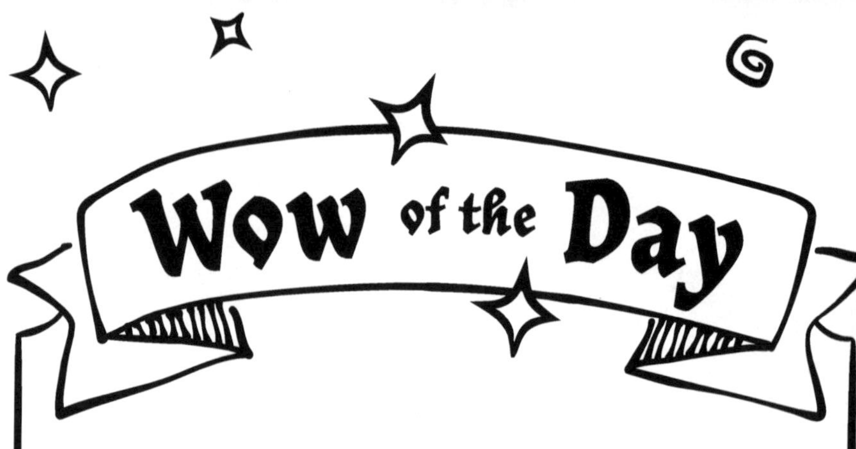

An entire set was built at Leavesden Film Studios to look like New York for the filming of *Fantastic Beasts and Where to Find Them,* but instead of tearing it down when the movie was finished, the studio decided to keep it. It remained and was used again for movies such as *Justice League.*

Magic Potions

Drink of the Four Houses

As nice as it is that everyone has their own strengths — when you combine a lot of good qualities, you get something even better! The drink of the four houses is a perfect example of this.

Ingredients for two glasses:

juice of 1 ½ oranges

some grenadine syrup

1 cup sparkling mineral water

some blue food coloring

Preparation:

First prepare two large glasses. Fill them about half full with the orange juice and then add some syrup. It is best to use a small spoon and let the syrup run slowly along the edge of the glass. This way, the colors will hardly mix, and you will get a yellow and a red layer.

Then color the sparkling water blue with the food coloring and carefully pour it into the glass (again, preferably with a spoon). You now have a green and a blue layer of color.

Now it's time to toast!

The work on the Diagon Alley set exceeded all of Rowling's expectations and even moved the author to tears when she visited.

There are almost no right angles in Diagon Alley. The roofs and walls of the houses are usually slightly crooked, which is why the name Diagon Alley is so appropriate.

The scenes in Diagon Alley were originally to be filmed in the streets of London. Later, however, it was decided to recreate the shopping street in the studio.

31

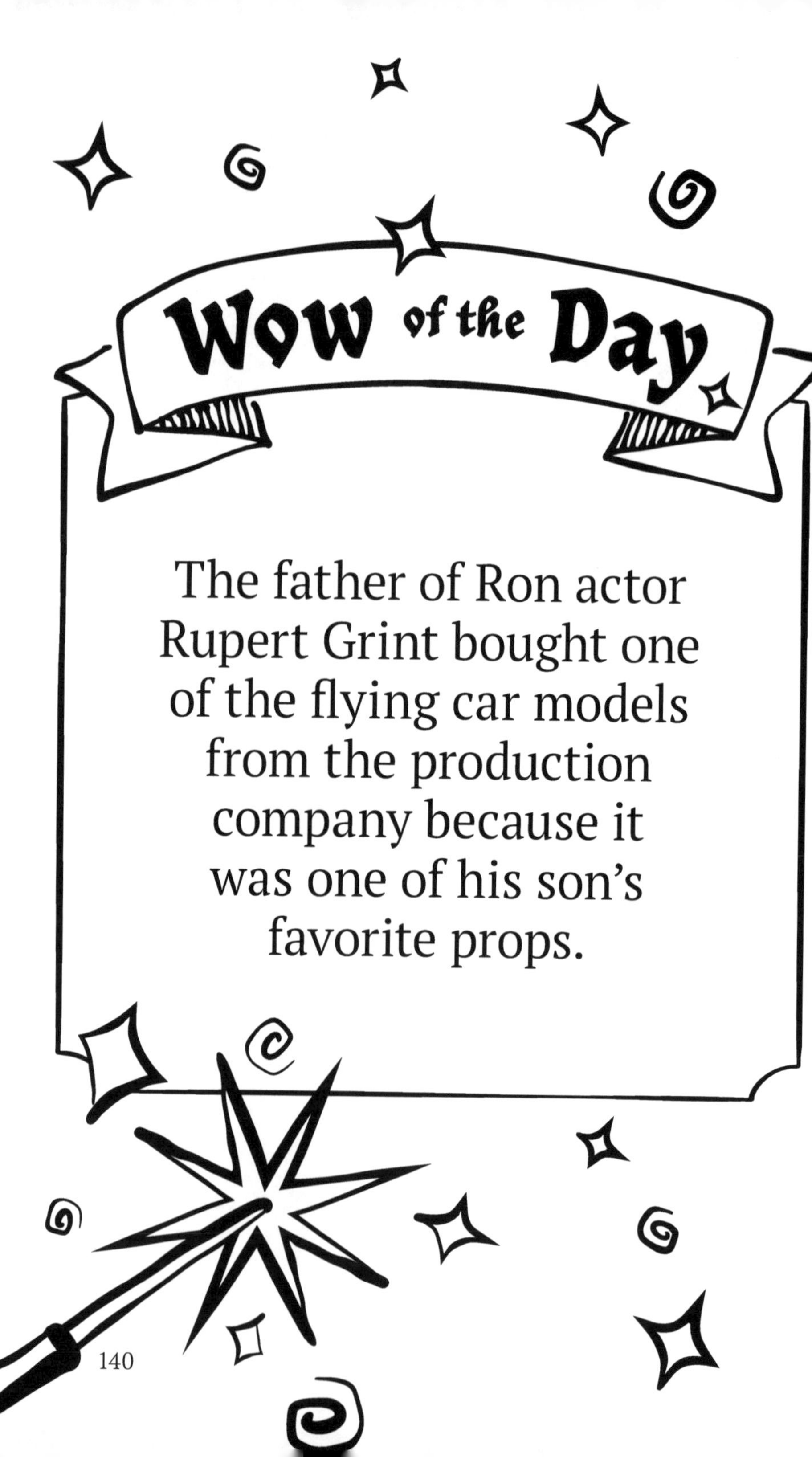

The father of Ron actor
Rupert Grint bought one
of the flying car models
from the production
company because it
was one of his son's
favorite props.

The Grand Finale

Tessomancy for Beginners

Although the art of divination can be learned at Hogwarts, not all witches and wizards have a knack for this supernatural gift. However, the basics can be learned by almost anyone — even some gifted Muggles.

To celebrate the turn of the year, you can practise this mysterious art yourself and give yourself, your friends, and your family some insights into the coming year. All you have to do is open yourself to mysticism and recognize the future in tea leaves.

All you need for a tea leaf reading ceremony is the following:

- ✦ a cup
- ✦ hot water
- ✦ loose tea (alternatively, cut open tea bags)

If you are a young wizard or witch — ask your parents for help with this. Pour one teaspoon of loose tea into your cup and then add hot water. Allow the tea to steep and cool.

The person whose fortune is to be told must then drink the tea until very little water remains at the bottom of the cup — and of course the tea leaves. If you want to tell your own fortune, simply drink the tea yourself.

This is where the magic comes in. If you are right-handed, hold the cup in your left hand; if you are left-handed, hold it in your right hand. Then swirl the cup and the water in it seven times and put it down again. Once the tea has settled, it's time to get a glimpse into the future.

Look into the cup from above, but don't move it anymore. What do you see? You may be able to recognize numbers, certain patterns and shapes, or even words.

Meanings

Here are some of the symbols you might come across and what they mean:

Anchor

Success awaits you

The anchor guarantees you stability in life. Stay exactly where you are, and success will follow.

Apple

An unexpected realization is to come

As the fruit of knowledge, the apple brings wisdom to the world. Now you will encounter a truth you never expected.

Axe

Danger ahead

The sharp edges of the axe indicate approaching danger. Keep your eyes open and your senses sharp.

Banana

Reach your goals

Have your goals felt as far away as a tropical island? Now they're within reach!

Bird

The solution to a problem

Like a bird, your problems will soar into the sky and disappear behind the horizon.

Blade

A painful experience is on the horizon

The sharper the blade, the cleaner the cut. However, this does not mean that an incisive experience cannot hurt.

Bottle

Take care of your health!

Make sure your health doesn't escape. Keep the top of your health bottle tightly closed.

Coin

A big win lies ahead

Gold or not — the coin has fallen, revealing a future filled with big wins.

Dog

The Grimm

The dark figure of the Grimm does not bode well. Prepare yourself for a difficult test!

Feather

A situation that requires sensitivity

You should be as delicate as the touch of a feather. Your next actions will determine the outcome of a situation.

Flag

A big announcement is coming

Like a waving flag, something big is looming on the horizon of the future. You are about to find out what it is.

Flower

A great love is waiting for you

The blossoming of a young love is one of the most beautiful things in life. Enjoy the spring fever — whatever the season!

Hat

A secret must be kept

Your knowledge lies undiscovered and secret. Make sure it remains hidden in the future.

House

Your hard work is paying off

Slowly and steadily, you are working towards your goals. Now it won't be long before your efforts are rewarded and the edifice of your ambition is complete.

Mountain

An obstacle to overcome

A steep climb is usually worth it. Climb to the top and then enjoy the view.

Pendulum

An important decision to make

Yes or no? Left or right? Center your thoughts and prepare yourself for a momentous decision.

Scissors

A confrontation awaits you

When the two sides of a pair of scissors meet, something is often destroyed. Sensitivity is therefore called for in this upcoming confrontation.

Ship

An unexpected encounter presents itself

Make room in your harbor of acquaintances. A new, previously unknown guest is expected.

Snake

You could be disappointed

Quickly and quietly, like a snake, a disappointment could creep into your life.

Square

Disaster can still be avoided

A change of direction can also take place in the mind. Such changes of course often lead to a positive resolution of a situation.

Tree

With a little time, happiness will blossom

The seed of happiness has already been planted. Now you must be patient for the fruit of your happiness to blossom.

Uncover More Incredible Secrets of the *Potter* World

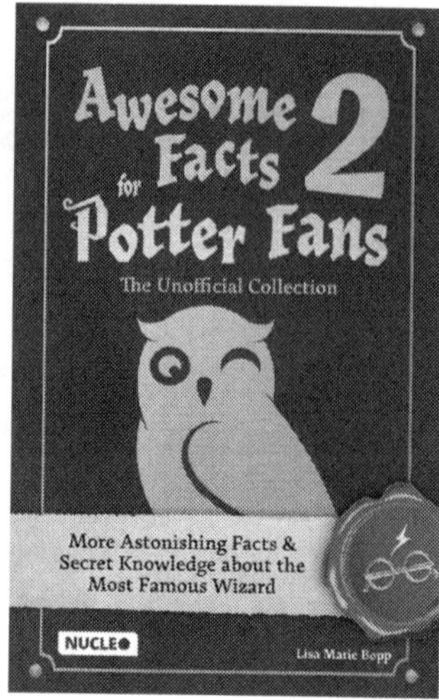

Did you know?

A main character was supposed to die early.

In the movies, Harry's glasses usually have no lenses at all.

In first thoughts, Harry had a different surname.

More magical facts & well-kept secrets are waiting for you!

Learn even more amazing things about the world's most famous wizard in a host of additional facts.

Volumes 1 and 2 of *Awesome Facts for Potter Fans* are available in stores.

Made in the USA
Middletown, DE
31 October 2024

63593652R00087